Dimensions of Ethnicity

A Series of Selections from the
Harvard Encyclopedia of American Ethnic Groups

Stephan Thernstrom, *Editor*
Ann Orlov, *Managing Editor*
Oscar Handlin, *Consulting Editor*

CONCEPTS OF ETHNICITY

WILLIAM PETERSEN
MICHAEL NOVAK
PHILIP GLEASON

The Belknap Press of
Harvard University Press
Cambridge, Massachusetts
London, England
1982

Library of Congress Cataloging in Publication Data

Main entry under title:

Concepts of ethnicity.

   (Dimensions of ethnicity)
   Selections from the Harvard encyclopedia of American ethnic groups.
   Bibliography: p.
   Contents: Concepts of ethnicity / William Peterson—Pluralism in
humanistic perspective / Michael Novak—American identity and
Americanization / Philip Gleason.
      1. Minorities—United States—Addresses, essays, lectures.
   2. Ethnicity—United States—Addresses, essays, lectures.
   3. Americanization—Addresses, essays, lectures.   4. Pluralism (Social
sciences)—Addresses, essays, lectures.   I. Petersen, William.   II. Novak,
Michael.   III. Gleason, Philip.   IV Title.   V. Series.
   E184.A1C58   1982   305.8'00973   82–6141
   ISBN 0–674–15726–5 (pbk.)   AACR2

Foreword

Ethnicity is a central theme—perhaps the central theme—of American history. From the first encounters between Englishmen and Indians at Jamestown down to today's "boat people," the interplay between peoples of differing national origins, religions, and races has shaped the character of our national life. Although scholars have long recognized this fact, in the past two decades they have paid it more heed than ever before. The result has been an explosive increase in research on America's complex ethnic mosaic. Examination of a recent bibliography of doctoral dissertations on ethnic themes written between 1899 and 1972 reveals that no less than half of them appeared in the years 1962–1972. The pace of inquiry has not slackened since then; it has accelerated.

The extraordinary proliferation of literature on ethnicity and ethnic groups made possible—and necessary—an effort to take stock. An authoritative, up-to-date synthesis of the current state of knowledge in the field was called for. The *Harvard Encyclopedia of American Ethnic Groups*, published by the Harvard University Press in 1980, is such a synthesis. It provides entries by leading scholars on the origins, history, and present situation of the more than 100 ethnic groups that make up the population of the United States, and 29 thematic essays on a wide range of ethnic topics. As one reviewer said, the volume is "a kind of *summa ethnica* of our time."

I am pleased that some of the most interesting and valuable articles in the encyclopedia are now available to a wider audience through inexpensive paperback editions such as this one. These essays will be an excellent starting point for anyone in search of deeper understanding of who the American people are and how they came to be that way.

Stephan Thernstrom

Contents

Concepts of Ethnicity

1
CONCEPTS OF ETHNICITY

The English language has often been enriched by the incorporation of more or less synonymous words from two or more sources. The many terms used in the analysis of ethnicity or nationalism, however, have not generally contributed to greater clarity. With so complex and contentious a topic, all designations have remained more or less ambiguous, and commentators are often unable to agree on the precise meaning of any of them. It might be useful in a fully authoritative piece to stipulate the "correct" meaning of each term; more realistically, the intent here is to trace the meanings assigned to each, beginning with its etymology and continuing through the connotations associated with it in various contexts.

Search for a Terminology

The word "ethnic" derives via Latin from the Greek *ethnikos*, the adjectival form of *ethnos*, a nation or race. As originally used in English, ethnic signified "not Christian or Jewish, pagan, heathen"; for example, in *The Leviathan* Thomas Hobbes exhorted Christian converts to continue obeying their "ethnic" rulers. "Nation" comes from Latin via French; its ultimate source is *nasci*, "to be born," and the closer source is *natio*, meaning originally "birth," later one of the barbarian tribes outside the Roman world.

The physiological association suggested by these etymologies was long retained in English, as we can see especially from some currently obsolete or rare usages. Like dozens of other words (such as "barbarian," meaning "not Greek") both "ethnic" and "nation" were applied originally to outsiders as a class. With the lessening of what we now term ethnocentrism, the range of many such words was extended from alien peoples to any people, including that of the speaker. And from their originally biological context, the meaning of both terms broadened to include cultural characteristics and political structures. But neither of these shifts has been consistent or unidirectional.

"Ethnic" is an adjective, and English never adopted a noun from the Greek *ethnos*. The lack of a convenient substantive form has induced writers to coin a number of makeshifts, all of which have their drawbacks. Of these, the commonest (as suggested by the title *Ethnic Encyclopedia*) is "ethnic group." Unfortunately, users of this term too often forget the crucial distinction between a group, which by definition has some degree of coherence and solidarity, and a subpopulation, category, grouping, aggregate, bracket, or sector, which denote no more than a patterned differentiation. The connotation of ethnic "group" is that its members are at least latently aware of common interests. Despite the difficulty of determining at what point people become a group, that is, the point at which coherence is established, it is important to retain the fundamental distinction between a group and a category, because many of the processes analyzed in the study of ethnic relations consist of the interaction between the two. Assimilation, thus, can be defined as movement from group to category, the rise of nationalism as movement in the other direction.

As professional jargon, "minority group" is even less suitable, for both its elements are ill chosen. According to Louis Wirth, whose writings did much to popularize the term, it refers simply to victims of a subordination that he condemned; "the people whom we regard as a minority may actually, from a numerical standpoint, be a majority." But in most of history, as well as in most of the non-Western world today, the dominant social division has been between a small ruling elite and a vast ruled mass; what Tocqueville called "the tyranny of the majority" can arise only in the exceptional democratic society. Wirth's term merely muddies, and thus facilitates a manipulation to fit the political occasion: in the British Isles the Irish are a widely dispersed minority; in all of Ireland the Protestants are a minority; in Northern Ireland the Catholics are a minority. Simply by drawing the appropriate boundary and stressing the self-serving portion of an area's history, partisans can almost always find a way to picture themselves as a victimized minority group.

In other works I have suggested the term "subnation," denoting simply a unit smaller than a nation but otherwise similar to it. A nation is a people linked by common descent from a putative ancestor and by its common territory, history, language, religion, or way of life. Obviously neither all nations nor all subnations conform to every element of this list, but the precise limits of subnations are often more difficult to fix because they are seldom directly associated with the counterpart of a boundary-protecting state. Hardly any other analysts have adopted "subnation" in place of the terms it was intended to supplant. One reason is that it also is ambiguous in suggesting that all of a nation's characteristics are typically shared by its ethnic parts.

The same difficulties are encountered in trying to fix the meanings of other derivatives from the word "nation." Originally "nationality" meant "national quality or character," then "a nation, frequently of a people potentially but not actually a nation." However, in the most common current usage in such multiethnic countries as the United States or the Soviet Union, it denotes a particular type of ethnic category. The words "nationalism" and "nationalist" can pertain to existent nations (in which case they are more or less equivalent to "patriotism" and "patriot"), but they are more likely to refer to ethnic sentiment with or without an implicit aspiration to establish an independent country: Polish nationalists want an independent Poland; Flemish nationalists want equal status with Walloons in a continuing Belgian state. It is unfortunate that we use the same word to designate both "black nationalism," most of whose advocates do not demand independence from the United States, and Canada's "French nationalism," whose leaders have demanded that the province of Quebec become a separate state. The term is especially imprecise in describing a shift from one level of group consciousness to another. In multiethnic Austria-Hungary, for instance, the creators of a new Slav awareness first demanded no more than greater group rights within the empire; only later did some of the Slav proponents begin to insist on independence for what eventually emerged as Czechoslovakia and Yugoslavia. And in such areas as black Africa today, it is less an analytic than a political judgment whether the surviving "tribalism" (or, in India, "communalism") expresses dissent within an essentially unified entity or the strivings of real nations to throw off the dominance of alien rulers.

Interpretation is likely to falter also when words in other languages are translated as "ethnicity" or "nationalism." This is the case even among the closely related western European languages. The French word *nation* has the same double meaning as its English derivative, either a community based on common characteristics or a political unit. A biological linkage is likely to be expressed by *peuple*, "people," and a territorial or sentimental one by *patrie*, "fatherland." The word *état*, "state," has the convenient derivatives *étatisme* and *étatisation*, which are rendered far less appropriately in English by "nationalism" (as in "economic nationalism") and "nationalization." Under the Nazi German program to delete all foreign words, *Nation*, which had usually implied a cultural rather than a political unit, was largely supplanted by *Volk*, very roughly, "people," but in fact untranslatable. The adjective *völkisch* denoted the essential, organic character of Germans, usually including more than those who were then living in the Reich. Since 1945 both *Volk* and *völkisch* have been used less, for they are considered tarnished by Nazism. French has a similar term, *ethnie*, to denote those bound by racial, cultural, and sentimental ties regardless of national boundaries; *l'ethnie française* thus comprises the French-speaking sectors not only of France but also of Belgium, Switzerland, Italy, and so on. According to Guy Héraud's *L'Europe des ethnies*, however, "each such population always represents, either actually or potentially, an *ethnie* also in the subjective sense—a nationality."

Ethnie is a neologism not yet included in general French dictionaries, and it may be that English will solve the terminological dilemma by adopting as a suitable noun either *ethnie* or the Greek *ethnos* or, most probably, "ethnic" itself. In recent popular writing it has been used as a substantive, usually applied only to certain categories: "white ethnics" are Italians and Poles, for example, but usually not Scots and Norwegians. If the meaning of the noun became comprehensive, like that of the adjective, and if the usage did not remain substandard, "ethnic" might be the most suitable term.

Ethnos versus Race

Of the various criteria of ethnicity, race is in many respects the most significant; the characteristics of the body, that most palpable element of one's persona, have been used throughout history to define the most pervasive type of group identity. Since *ethnos* with its derivatives pertained originally to a biological grouping, it was close to our "race" (probably derived from *ratio*, which in medieval Latin was used to designate species). In its current usage a biological connotation sometimes adheres still to "ethnic," but not necessarily: some groupings are defined by their genetic heritage, others by their language or religion or some other criterion. Apart from poetry or metaphor, "race" in English has referred consistently to a biological unit, but its size has varied from a family line (as in Tennyson's "We were two daughters of one race") to the entire species (as in "the human race"). Indeed, as physical anthropologists use the term, the size of a race depends simply on the purpose of the particular investigator: it denotes a subpopulation that differs significantly from others in the frequency of one or more genes, with "significantly" specified according to the context. Its cognates in other European languages—French *race*, German *Rasse,* and so on—are still used with a seeming indifference to either the range of the unit or the amount of difference between it and other subpopulations. English, however, has shown a trend toward what would be a useful distinction, reserving "race" for mankind's major biological divisions and using another designation for smaller groupings within it. Thus, many American writers now distinguish "racial" from "ethnic" minorities, the former being Negroes, Asians, and other "nonwhites," the latter the European nationalities.

The separation of the two terms has been inhibited, however, by the confusion in real life between physiological and cultural criteria. Very often a racial group is set off from the rest of the population by cultural characteristics as well; conversely, if the endogamy enjoined or at least encouraged by most religious faiths and other cultural groups continues for enough generations, it is likely to result in a perceptible physical differentiation. In a Mexican census enumeration, following that country's usual perception of its ethnic pattern, an "Indian" is one who speaks an Indian language and wears Indian clothing; if he learns to speak Spanish and shifts from huaraches to shoes, he becomes a "mestizo." The stereotype that an Indian is unable to perform industrial tasks is not only true but a truism: a factory worker is no longer an Indian.

In the aftermath of the Nazi program of genocide, a number of anthropologists have argued that we should delete "race" from our languages, not only because it is associated with racism but fundamentally because it is a vague category with imprecise and shifting boundaries. Whether the removal of a word would also eradicate group antipathies is doubtful; one suspects that with another classification Jews and Gypsies would have been murdered just as bestially. In any case, deleting the term does not remove the need for some designation. Ashley Montagu, who has argued the case most vociferously, suggested that "ethnic group" be substituted for "race," but the consequent confusion of biological and cultural characteristics, paradoxically, is the hallmark of racism. Whether Jews constitute the "race" (or, to use a common euphemism, "stock") that the Nazis asserted them to be depends on the context. In a discussion of religious or other cultural characteristics, genetic make-up is manifestly irrelevant, but in a study of dysautonomia, a genetic disease especially prevalent among Jews, the crucial factor is precisely their hereditary links. Moreover, the notion that only "pure" categories may be admitted to exist is bizarre; it follows from the theory of evolution itself that all biological divisions, from phylum through subspecies, are always in the process of change, so there is almost never a sharp and permanent boundary setting one off from the next.

Culturally Defined Groupings

If the demand for pure categories were to be extended to the indicators generally used in the social disciplines, acceding to it would bar most research. For the difference is also partly arbitrary, and thus more or less mutable, between, say, the rural and the urban, the employed and the unemployed, the literate and the illiterate, and so on. As Abraham Kaplan put it in his classic *The Conduct of Inquiry*, "It is the dogmatisms outside science that proliferate closed systems of meaning; the scientist is in no hurry for closure. Tolerance of ambiguity is as important for creativity in science as it is anywhere else."

The meaning of "language," probably the second most prevalent indicator of ethnicity, is as ambiguous as that of "race." Forms of speech known to be related constitute what is known as a "linguistic stock," made up of what are deemed to be languages and what are called dialects. But with the advance of knowledge, the Germanic stock, for example, was recognized as a subunit of the larger Indo-European stock. As Edward Sapir put it in his standard work on linguistics, the terms dialect, language, branch, and stock are all only relative, convertible as our perspective widens or contracts.

Often linguistic characteristics matter less in determining the designation than the cultural or political status of the subpopulation that uses a particular speech. Flemish was once the "dialect" of Dutch spoken in Belgium, but now, after the successful effort of Flemish nationalists to establish it as such, Flemish or "Southern Dutch" is one of the country's two official "languages." Romansch, comprising several dialects spoken by tiny remnants of some Roman legions, was elevated in 1938 to the fourth official language of Switzerland. Perhaps the strangest case is the recent acceptance of a second language, Landsmål, in Norway, a country with some 4 million inhabitants and one of the few in the world that until then had not manifested any significant ethnic differentiation. Because the standard speech used by the educated middle class was close to Danish, agitation for recognition of the new language was based in part on "patriotism"; and because Landsmål, an amalgam of several dialects, is spoken by peasants and fishermen, a second appeal could be made based on "democracy." After more than a century of accelerating agitation, the proponents of a second official Norwegian language achieved their purpose, and today the country's schoolchildren must learn both.

The meaning of "region," another ethnic indicator, is also

far from clear-cut. Sometimes it is based on what is termed a "natural area," that is, a physiographic unit delineated by its topography, soil type, climate, or similar features. Particularly among primitive peoples, who have relatively little control over their physical environment, a natural area may overlap within what anthropologists call a "culture area," which approaches what we ordinarily think of as a region. The U.S. Bureau of the Census divides the United States into four regions (Northeast, North Central, South, and West), with each subdivided into "geographic divisions." These designations developed only gradually and remain somewhat arbitrary; whether there actually are subcultures associated with New England, the Midwest, and so on depends in large part on where one draws the boundaries and which indexes one uses to measure the supposed differences.

In short, none of the group characteristics—whether cultural or physical—that are used to denote ethnicity generally set off any subpopulation sharply. A great contrast is likely only when several indexes overlap. In Canada, for example, the French-speaking sector resides mostly in the province of Quebec, is Catholic rather than Protestant like most other Canadians, and—to add a nonethnic factor—was until recently concentrated in the lower and lower-middle classes in contrast with the English-speaking employers and professionals in the province. The world-famous amity of the Swiss, on the other hand, has been partly based on the happy accident that the lines of ethnic division have cut across one another. The main emotional issue in 19th-century Switzerland was religion; then it became nationality, with each of the three main language communities speaking a tongue in common with a contiguous foreign country. But both the German- and French-speaking Swiss are both Catholic and Protestant; opposed in one arena, they have always been aware that they would be allies in another. Moreover, the proportions of German-, French-, and Italian-speaking Swiss were constant for more than a century, so that no one had to fear the day that a minority would reach the fateful 51 percent—when any modus vivendi that had been worked out would become obsolete.

Official Counts of Ethnic Groups

The vagaries of ethnic classification are especially apparent in the several United Nations comparisons of the criteria used in the world's censuses. According to the first of these compilations, in 1957, 39 countries divided their populations by a geographical-ethnic criterion, 10 by race, 8 by culture, 22 by a combination of race and culture, 11 by a combination of culture and geography, one or two by origin as indicated by the language of the respondent's father, and several by "mode of life." Even when the same term was used, the meaning sometimes was different. Replies to questions on matters reflecting social prestige were probably often false. And the enumerations have not improved since this initial comparison.

If the subnations of any society are classified only partly according to their objective characteristics, how are the non-objective criteria set? Most obviously, they are chosen to fit the view that the politically dominant grouping has of the whole, and invariably one of the principal dimensions divides "insiders," variously defined, from "outsiders." In the United States, for example, "English American" occasionally has been defined as one nationality among others, and the census bureau tabulates persons with English-born parents or grandparents as part of the "foreign stock"; more generally, those with English forebears have been regarded as the core population with which others have been compared. In other circumstances the dominant group may be given the most statistical attention. American whites are divided by nationality, but Americans of other races are considered single entities—though in a Negro community the distinction is just as significant between a southern and a West Indian background, or in a Japanese community between origin in the main islands and in Okinawa. On the other hand, American Indians are enumerated by tribe, including even very small ones, and in Hawaii a count has been made of the perhaps 2 percent of the population listed as pure Polynesian, though most in that category are actually part-Hawaiians who claimed unmixed ancestry in order to gain special access to schooling, homesteads, certain occupations, and other opportunities.

In the continuous interplay among groups, any answer to the question of how they shall be designated seldom remains fixed. The formal names of those low in an ethnic hierarchy, recurrently seen as derogatory, are repeatedly replaced with one synonym or another. When the National Association for the Advancement of Colored People (NAACP) was founded at the beginning of the 20th century, the only fully acceptable term for Negroes was "colored"; "negro," "Negro," "Afro-American," "black," and "Black" —terms that sectors of the Negro population have successively insisted on—were then regarded as insulting. Several groups of Negro-Indian-white ancestry in the southern Appalachians successfully demonstrated against their enumeration as "Negro" and were reclassified as "Indian." On the other hand, a decision *not* to classify a population along a particular dimension, though it is typically justified by an assertion that the differentiation is unimportant, may be based rather on a reluctance to publicize significant ethnic-class or ethnic-political correlations. For example, when the U.S. Bureau of the Census suggested including a question on religious affiliation in the 1960 schedule, the opposition from Jewish organizations was so strong that the proposal was dropped.

An important influence on any classificatory system, finally, is the convenience of the administrative agency that makes the count. The census bureau is under heavy and often conflicting pressures, and the choice between monetary or other costs and its assessment of national utility has varied from time to time. Since 1890, the first year that all Indians were counted, the inclusiveness of the definition has shifted from one census to the next, so that the total enumeration has fluctuated. The money-saving procedure of dividing printed tables into only two categories, "whites" and "nonwhites," makes sense for areas where nonwhite is virtually equivalent to Negro, but not in the Southwest or Hawaii, where substantial percentages are Chinese, Japanese, American Indian, or Polynesian. The trend from a *de jure* to a *de facto* definition of residence has also affected reported counts of particular areas. The decision, for instance, to include members of the armed forces and their dependents in the population of Hawaii—a choice no less arbitrary than to exclude them—substantially altered not only the state's racial proportions but also the reported age structure, mortality, fertility, income level, and so on through the whole range of demographic and social data.

In sum, ethnic differentiation is typically both important and imprecise. Paradoxically, an impressionistic account of how one ethnic sector is set off from others can be more accurate than one based on sharp divisions. In law and demography, however, an absolute demarcation is almost inescapable. If members of certain minorities are given preferential access to colleges and jobs through "affirmative action," precise criteria for eligibility are necessary. And a census that reports the race or nationality of every individual in the society leaves no place for miscellany. Like most other social indicators, ethnic ones are likely to transform the stupendous complexity of our world into a more comprehensible simplicity, and much of what we think we know about ethnicity derives from such statistics.

Processes of Assimilation

The shorthand denotation of the prevailing belief early in this century was that America is a "melting pot." In later attacks on this symbol of total assimilation, it was often forgotten that the slogan derived from a play written by Israel

Zangwill, paying homage to "the great Alchemist [who] melts and fuses them with his purging flame—Celt and Latin, Slav and Teuton, Greek and Syrian," and, as represented in the play's hero and heroine, Jew and Gentile. The melting pot was probably an accurate metaphor for the insecure first generation's aspiration to disappear totally, to merge into indistinguishable sameness with "real" Americans.

At that time placing restrictions on immigration was a crucial political issue. If all immigrants were indeed developing into identical American citizens, then obviously the xenophobic demands of restrictionists were not well based. Academic leaders gave ideological support to this antirestrictionist argument. According to the most important social theorist of the 1920s, Professor Robert E. Park of the University of Chicago, all interethnic relations go through an invariable and irreversible four-stage succession of contact, competition, accommodation, and assimilation. Progress along this line is inevitable—except when some factor interferes with it temporarily. Once its premises are accepted, the schema is unassailable; the many ethnic groups that have remained distinct for decades (or centuries) can always be explained by special circumstances, and the dogma that full amalgamation will be attained "eventually" remains intact. In two respects Park went beyond even Zangwill's extravagantly utopian view. He generalized the vista to all peoples; as he wrote, "the melting pot is the world." And in the United States, Park was mainly concerned not with European nationalities but with races, whose differences were etched in law and in seemingly strong and unchanging sentiment.

This view of race relations in the United States was adopted in Gunnar Myrdal's *An American Dilemma* (1944), still the major synthesis of works on its topic. In a hundred contexts, Myrdal and his collaborators argued that all but the most superficial differences between whites and blacks derived from white prejudice and discriminatory institutions. As one example of a vicious circle leading to a pattern of mutually supporting elements, racially segregated schools derived from the whites' belief that Negroes are genetically of inferior intelligence, and products of the poorer Negro schools often validated the thesis that on the average Negroes are indeed more stupid. For the common phrase "vicious circle," Myrdal substituted his own term, the "principle of cumulation," for he wanted to emphasize that the process could work in either direction. If those who did not accept racist dogma demanded the desegregation of education (and the *Brown* decision of the Supreme Court was delivered only a decade after *An American Dilemma* was published), then the Negroes who consequently got a better schooling would erode the belief in genetic differences in intelligence, and gradually all significant distinctions between the races would disappear.

A high point in American views of acculturation was reached in Milton Gordon's *Assimilation in American Life* (1964), which incorporated the thesis of "cultural pluralism" developed by Horace Kallen and provided a much more cautious analysis than the academic version of the melting pot. Desegregation, Gordon held, need not lead "immediately" or "necessarily" to the integration of ethnic communities, but he made the point mainly in order to quell the fear of "die-hard segregationists" that the granting of civil rights would result in widespread intermarriage. To the "built-in tension between the goals of ethnic communality and desegregation" there seemed to be no solution except good will on the part of all.

With such works American sociologists gave an aura of verisimilitude to the vista of a future either without meaningful ethnicity or at least with little or no ethnic conflict. In spite of its now manifest faults, this American theory (as we might term it) has been influential in other countries whose history has been shaped by immigration, such as Australia. European analysts were more likely to be concerned about how to *prevent* assimilation—how language communities, for instance, could maintain their identity and prevent what the Nazis termed *Gleichschaltung* (which can be inadequately translated as "homogenization"). And social scientists everywhere have been influenced by Marx, reflecting both his lack of interest in nationalism and ethnicity and his certainty that these primordial sentiments, remnants of a past age, had survived beyond their term.

The Rise of Ethnicity

To most analysts of ethnic relations, the worldwide rise of racial, religious, linguistic, or nationalist sentiment—and often violent opposition to it—came as a surprise. Why, contrary to almost every informed opinion, have recent years seen a reassertion of ethnicity? Only a few strands of the complex answer to this question can be offered here.

First, one should note that almost all the earlier doctrines —whether the melting pot or Marxism—typically evolved as support for a political position rather than as a purely objective analysis of the trend in interethnic relations. Even as ethnic identity was becoming more significant in the United States, attempts were being made, in conformance with national policy, to disguise the very existence of racial differences. Such pressure groups as the American Civil Liberties Union tried to have the question on race deleted from the 1960 census schedule, and for one year New Jersey actually did omit race and color from its birth and death certificates. Following the prestigious example of the *New York Times*, many newspapers left out racial identifications of all persons on whom they reported. Various states passed laws stipulating that applications for employment or for entrance to college and similar forms could not require an ethnic identification or a photograph, which was considered an approximate equivalent. These procedures were all based on the premise that an official recognition of ethnic (and particularly racial) differentiation facilitated discrimination, but even in the context in which they were proposed they were inept. It was hardly possible to evaluate the many experimental programs designed to raise the status of blacks, for example, without data on race. And the subsequent change to new imperatives came so quickly that universities, for example, were for a time simultaneously forbidden to record the race of their faculty and students and required to report what proportions of each were of specified minorities. One reason that rising ethnicity burst on us with such startling suddenness was the earlier effort to combat racism by omitting race, religion, and nationality from public records.

A parallel stance was common in the analysis of prejudice. Literally, "prejudice" means prejudgment, a judgment before knowledge. In Theodore Newcomb's *Social Psychology* (1950), then one of the dominant texts in the field, prejudice was defined as "an unfavorable attitude—a predisposition to perceive, act, think, and feel in ways that are 'against' rather than 'for' another person or group," contrasted with a "predisposition toward intimacy and/or helpfulness." In the authoritative *Handbook of Social Psychology* (1954), as another instance, the term was defined as "an ethnic attitude in which the reaction tendencies are predominantly negative . . . simply an unfavorable ethnic attitude." Ostensibly any hostile judgment concerning any group was denounced, but of course this was not the case. The substitution of adverse judgment for prejudgment was itself a political stand.

The negativism included blocking out scholarly works with a different point of view. Paradoxically, America's first outstanding analysis of ethnicity, William Graham Sumner's *Folkways* (1906), was in some respects the most perceptive. Terms that Sumner introduced—"folkways" itself, "mores," "ethnocentrism," "in-group," "out-group," and so on—became common usage in subsequent works, but no trace remained of his belief that group differences, because they are based on distinctions seen to be more or less immutable, are likely to persevere. One cannot change the mores, he wrote, "by any artifice or device, to a great extent, or suddenly, or in any essential element . . . Changes which are opposed to the mores require long and patient effort, if they are possible at all."

Second, the assumption that assimilation, however fast or slow, is a one-way process proved to be quite mistaken. Marcus Lee Hansen's hypothesis of "third-generation nationalism" showed an unusually shrewd appreciation of assimilation by picturing it as a cycle, with marked differences between immigrants, their children, and their grandchildren. The national churches, immigrant-aid societies, foreign-language newspapers, and other institutions that the first generation set up were not impediments to acculturation but generally the contrary. The manifest difficulties of the second generation derived from "the strange dualism into which they had been born," and they tried to solve it by escaping the stigma they saw attached to their alien lineage. The immigrants' sons "wanted to lose as many of the evidences of foreign origin as they could shuffle off." But what the son wanted to forget, the grandson wanted to remember. Approximately 60 years—that is, two generations—after the high point of each nationality's immigration, the ethnic group into which it evolved typically celebrated its origins in a succession of amateur historical and genealogical societies, folklore associations, and other organized efforts to maintain or revive specific elements of various overseas cultures. Hansen's thesis, as he remarked in one place in the essay, was "deliberately overdrawn," and subsequent scholars have challenged its application to particular nationalities, but it can be regarded not only as a largely valid analysis of acculturation but also as a special case of a far broader social change.

In the transformation to a modernist, bureaucratic society, much is given up that eventually is regarded as valuable. Personal identity is very thin unless it is enmeshed with what Harold Isaacs calls the "idols of the tribe," the symbolic meanings given to group differences in body, name, language, history, religion, and nationality. It was hardly surprising, after all, that once the more pressing demands had been met, many tried to escape the impersonality of metropolitan life and retrogressively to establish a fuller emotional environment for themselves. Of course, the cycle was not precisely three generations long in every case. Zangwill, whose play was a prominent symbol of the first step, became an ardent Zionist later in his life. But apart from such details, it seems to be generally true that attempts to acculturate to the dominant population arise from an initial insecurity, and that from later security there develops in turn a yearning to distinguish one's group from the mass.

Because of their special circumstances, American blacks took several generations more to reach the attitudes that Hansen associated with the grandchildren of immigrants. A generation or two ago, most of the Negroes who succeeded in moving up the social ladder—painfully, step by step—imitated the lifestyle of middle-class whites, moving both physically and spiritually as far from the black slum as possible. The standard of feminine beauty, as a crucial example, comprised mainly a light skin and "good" hair. Having achieved a middle-range income, in short, the "black bourgeoisie" (as the Negro sociologist Franklin Frazier opprobriously labeled them) generally tried to consolidate their new status through acculturation to the norms of the superordinate sector. With the federal government's accelerated legal attack on discrimination during the 1960s, the exceptional advance of individual Negroes became more general. A measurement of the rise of the whole black race averages two quite distinct subgroups: those Negroes who took full advantage of the expanded opportunities and those who, because of age, region, or family structure, found it difficult or impossible to do so. If we control for these three factors, the income of whites and blacks was close to parity by the early 1970s. Nothing in the whole assimilationist doctrine, from Park's race-relations cycle to Myrdal's principle of cumulation, prepared Americans for what happened. The response to an improvement in the economic and civil condition of Afro-Americans greater than at any time since Reconstruction was a massive resurgence of black separatism, led sometimes by the very men who had moved up farthest and fastest.

Third, it would be fanciful to suppose, however, that the rise of ethnicity in the United States and throughout most of the world was owing solely to a postponed search for roots. Obviously more is at stake than sentiment.

Even when it was fashionable to deny the relevance of race, religion, and nationality in national politics, this myth could hardly be applied with even minimum plausibility to America's multiethnic cities. In their relation to the federal government, voters were supposed to act as ethnically undifferentiated Americans, but in a metropolitan context they obviously and unabashedly constituted ethnic units— partly, of course, because an openly double ethnic identity was seen as a sensitive issue in national politics. The principal reason for the contrast between nation and city, however, was that by their functions local governments could distribute jobs, contracts, licenses, access to facilities, and so on. In order to get preferential treatment from a ward boss, a person had to join with others into a smaller, less blunt wedge than the heterogeneous national political parties, and one obvious base for mustering such power lay in the already existent, quasi-political, ethnically based clubs or churches.

With the New Deal there began a continuous, often accelerating, transfer to Washington of multitudinous local or private functions, all of them associated with special favors to particular sectors of the population. With its version of the welfare state, the United States moved closer to the European norm, which eventually was imitated everywhere. The worldwide rise of ethnicity is based, in other words, not only on what Robert Nisbet called the "quest for community" but also, and more importantly, on the wider functions of the state and thus the greater impetus to organize in order to get what the state is distributing—and to prevent others from getting it.

The Origins of Ethnic Groups

Even if we postulate the only half-effective melting pot that critics of Zangwill's original formulation seem to have substituted, we must ask how (rather than why) it is that ethnicity has become a more and more important organizing principle. The conventional American view of ethnic relations is that subnations come into being mainly—or even only—through migration, but relative to the world's population, generally only small proportions have migrated. The dilemma is similar to that faced by pre-Darwinian exponents of biology: all species had been brought into being only once, at the time of the world's creation; some had disappeared, as was known from their fossil remains, but the number of species in the world seemed to be growing. Darwin resolved the dilemma by describing how new species arise, and it is also necessary, on a more modest scale, to consider the origins of ethnic groups and the process by which they emerge—ethnogenesis. The examples are drawn from American society except when the types can be illustrated only from other parts of the world.

Migration

In the long and often disputatious discussion of how immigrants relate to American culture, some interesting analytical points have been largely ignored. It is not true that one can judge the impact of Swedish immigrants, for example, by comparing the cultures of Sweden and the United States; migrants are almost never a random sample of the populations they leave and enter. In this instance, since most emigrants were neither urban nor upper-class, they took with them not the general culture of Sweden but rather a peasant variant, expressed in local dialects and comprising regional customs. Free migrants, moreover, are generally already half-assimilated even before leaving home; before someone left to go to a Swedish-American settlement, he started his acculturation in an American-Swedish milieu, made up of New World letters, photographs, mementos, knickknacks—all stimuli to what was termed "America fever." In order to understand fully the interaction between migrants and a host population, therefore, one should conduct research at both ends of the movement, but of the many scholars of migration to the United States, only two men in their generation manifestly satisfied this requirement—Marcus Lee Hansen for emigrants from northwestern Europe and Melville Herskovits for the movement of slaves from West Africa.

One characteristic of immigration that U.S. analysts often take for granted is that the receiving population is sufficiently large, powerful, and cultured to act as a "host" to newcomers. In contrast to this pattern, the Jewish population of Israel in the early 1970s included about half who had not been born in the country, and fewer than a tenth were natives with native-born fathers. During the decades following the establishment of the nation in 1948, acculturation was thus not to a host population but rather to the ideology of Zionism. As another example, immigration accounted for 58 percent of the population growth of Argentina over the century 1841–1940 (compared with 41 percent in the United States, 22 percent in Canada, and 19 percent in Brazil). More importantly, immigrants became Argentina's modernizing force, the major constituent of both the urban proletariat (as in the United States) and the urban middle class. The complexities of Argentina's politics, reflecting the rapid and anomalous shifts in the social structure, are related to the only partial integration of an unprecedentedly high proportion of the well-to-do foreign-born in the country's population.

Consolidation

According to a compilation by the anthropologists Charles and Florence Voegelin, at the time of Columbus's voyages the Indians of North America spoke a total of 221 mutually unintelligible languages, not including some contiguous dialects that permitted a minimal communication. Such other basic cultural elements as means of subsistence, religion, and family organization also varied greatly, and the differences were aggravated by a long history of violent competition and institutionalized warfare. Not only the name "Indian" but also the concept of a single people was a product of white contact. Even so, Indians might have become a single ethnic minority in the American population except for various federal policies, in particular the Indian Reorganization Act of 1934, that reinforced the atomized structure by giving tribal leaders a much enhanced power. The intermittent efforts to establish an intertribal movement have been fostered mostly by young men alienated as much from tribal life as from the white middle class. Over the next generation or two, the aspirations of many—probably most —younger Indians to participate fully in the world beyond the reservation will probably be realized. The decline of tribal units is likely to promote the rise of a new ethnic group, based ostensibly on cultural remnants that its members half-recall, but more fundamentally on the benefits obtainable from today's ethnic politics.

Inhabitants of the Appalachian Mountains provide another example of consolidation-in-process. Like the American Indians, their past relations with one another have been hostile; residents of each hamlet, huddled in its narrow valley, perceived those from over the mountain as unwelcome strangers. Also as with Indians, the isolated pockets of humanity were first defined as a single entity from the outside, especially by those in federal agencies set up to combat the region's poverty. A wide range of organizations and institutions is now active in promoting the subculture of "the Mountain People," and the consequent consolidation may have been assisted by their increased contacts with others and their greater awareness that those who live in the Appalachian region are distinct. It is at least possible, as it is probable for Indians, that their further acculturation to the general society will be by the circuitous route of uniting into a firmer and more self-conscious subculture.

Promotion

As we have noted in the case of Norway, raising a dialect to the status of a language can shift a lower social class to parity on an ethnic scale. In the United States the rise of "black English" suggests a similar process, though at a far earlier stage. The trend has been to define the black subculture not as standard American culture truncated by educational deprivation but as an immigrant way of life with significant transfers from Africa, and accordingly some have now defined the speech of lower-class blacks as a genuine dialect. It is said to have derived in large part from the pidgin English developed along Africa's west coast (as with Swahili along the east coast) for the greater convenience of the slave traders. Some students of black English advocate merely that it be used in elementary grades as a convenient bridge to learning English, but others have proposed that clergymen, for instance, become "bilingual," preaching in the parishioners' language and communicating with the broader community in standard English. In other words, the typically long process has been collapsed: even before a lower-class argot has been generally recognized as a dialect, some have begun to insist that it is in fact a language. Afro-Americans constituted a distinct ethnic group earlier, of course, but the usual academic position a generation ago was to ascribe their cultural differences almost entirely to their lower-class status.

Schism

In the alternation between sect and church—that is, between a small group espousing unadorned doctrine and the end product of its gradual embellishment with ritual and institutional form—there are repeated schisms. Sometimes the differentiation, though at first defined in religious terms, broadens to include a whole way of life, with the consequent formation of a new ethnic group. The Latter-day Saints, or Mormons, might be so regarded. In the 19th century dozens of new religions and secular communal settlements blossomed in New York, Pennsylvania, and Ohio, but almost all except the Mormons disappeared. The crucial difference may have been persecution, for nothing is so likely to nourish a new religion as the martyrdom of its leaders. The long trek to Utah (celebrated in partisan accounts as are those of the Boers in South Africa or of the Chinese Communists' "Long March") eventually brought about the Mormons' partial isolation, though not an end to hostility. Under two acts of Congress, polygamy was prohibited, the church lost its corporate status, with its property escheated to the nation, and men with more than one wife were disfranchised and imprisoned. This renewed martyrdom reinforced the devotion of the faithful, and even after polygamy was abandoned in 1890, relations with "Gentiles" did not improve greatly. Contrary to the constitutional principle of separation of powers, church and state for Mormons were joined in what outsiders saw as a theocracy. Suffrage in Utah meant that church members elected religious leaders, who also became the heads of civil government. In short, even after the issue of polygamy was long past, even after the isolation of their desert home was breached by greatly improved transportation, the Mormons remained a distinct group, now set apart less by their religious doctrine than by the social-political organizations associated with the church.

Race Crossing

In many works on ethnicity what is termed "amalgamation" is denoted as one major route to the formation of new groups. American history challenges the validity of this thesis in at least some instances. Afro-Americans have a high proportion of white forebears, but apart from the very few who have passed into the white population, the group as a whole has been defined in law and general perceptions as one race, regardless of the degree of admixture. As a second example, sociologists in Hawaii have retained the melting-pot theory as a guide to their thinking far longer than the rest of the country, and one reads again and again that a new composite race is developing on the islands. Even if this were so biologically, it is an unlikely social prognosis. The Chinese in Hawaii, for instance, have set up Chinese-language schools for their children and made other efforts to maintain their separate subculture, even though probably a majority carry a great many Polynesian and other non-Chinese genes.

The Cape Colored of South Africa, in contrast to American Negroes, do constitute a separate subnation that was brought into being by race crossing. They have no tribal homelands; they are not tribally organized; they speak mostly Afrikaans rather than a language of one of the black peoples. For many years they had a separate juridical status, different from that of both whites and blacks, and vestiges of their intermediate status remain in certain occupational or residential privileges. In other words, the Cape Colored became a separate ethnic group not by race crossing alone but by this combined with a number of sociopolitical institutions that set them apart.

By one or more of these processes—migration, consolidation, promotion, schism, and race crossing—new ethnic groups are continually coming into being. The development is generally through three stages—category, group, and community. A category consists of a subpopulation distinguished in a census count, say, but with no internal coherence. An example might be "Canadian Americans," people born in Canada and resident in the United States; the English-speaking ones, at least, are not organized along ethnic lines and probably have little knowledge even of one another's existence. From such a base, however, an ethnic group can arise, particularly at a time when the self-awareness of others leads to preferential treatment of various kinds. Often there is considerable difficulty in defining a nascent group's precise dimensions. The "Spanish-speaking" or "Hispanic" grouping includes immigrants from Spain and some of their descendants—Mexican Americans, Puerto Ricans, Cuban refugees, and contingents from other Central and South American countries. Whether such a conglomerate can merge to form a single, self-conscious group may depend on such extraneous factors as the quality of leadership, the advantages of corporate effort as against intercategory competition, and so on. But if a group coalesces and prospers, it often develops enough of an institutional structure to be deemed a community. Sometimes, however, the progression from category to group to community is blocked or reversed by the contrary process of assimilation. Neither differentiation nor its opposite is ordained, and we know too little even to say which is more likely under specified conditions. No one, however, will any longer challenge the generalization that ethnicity is here to stay for quite a number of years; and that, strangely, is a new datum.

2
PLURALISM IN HUMANISTIC PERSPECTIVE

Humanists have not analyzed as closely as they should the concept of ethnicity. By and large, this task has been left to scholars in the fields of history, political science, and sociology. This essay, therefore, may appear to offer a novel view of the subject. Scholars, teachers, and writers in the fields of literature, philosophy, and theology do have resources to bring to bear upon the realities of ethnicity, not only as these have affected human life in the past, but primarily as these affect the present—and promise to affect the future—under the rubric of the "new ethnicity." These resources have not yet been fully differentiated and sharpened. Scholars in the humanities commonly work upon literary texts, public rituals and liturgies, manners, mores, and ethical practices. The empirical clarity available to social scientists is theirs only at secondhand. But what they can do—and what this essay undertakes—is to ferret out the ways by which the daily realities of ethnicity are felt and perceived in ordinary experience, and to establish the worldviews within which such experiences are daily understood.

A theory about the methods proper to the humanities may help to orient the reader. The humanities are concerned about the question, "Who?" They are concerned about the human person, the human subject, and thus about the experiencing, perceiving, imagining, understanding, judging, and deciding of human persons. *Quidquid percipitur,* runs the Thomistic adage, *per modum percipientis percipitur: Whatever is perceived is perceived through the character of the one who perceives.* Who a person is (the range and quality of his or her experiences, imaginings, understandings, decidings, etc.) affects what a person perceives. The scientist is taught to operate in the mode of objectivity, discounting so much as is possible the factor of *whoness. Any* observer trained to the scientific mode should be able to replace the original observer, without loss of meaning. Subjectivity, so far as is possible, is eliminated. In the humanities, by contrast, students are trained to deepen and to enlarge their own subjectivity, to attempt to "cross over" and to enter into the subjectivity of others. They are taught that subjectivity is, in human affairs, important; that it is finally irreplaceable; and that it holds within it much that repays the effort to raise questions in order to understand more exactly. The work of scientists sometimes seems almost mystical to humanists, containing as it does measurements, lucid analytical models, mathematical invention of great brilliance, and refined and much-tested verbal clarity. Similarly, the work of humanists must seem, at times, almost mystical to scientists, with its indirect ways of eliciting almost unconscious senses of reality (myths), symbols, stories, viewpoints, sensibilities, images, and imaginal structures. Necessarily, humanists must discuss ethnicity in a way unfamiliar to, and at least in part unsatisfactory to, the scientist. Still, the work of the humanist is valuable to the scientist, if only to provoke further inquiry by turning up surprises, puzzles, anomalies, or perhaps even wholly new paradigms within which to raise further questions. For the scientist, too, and not only part time, is a human being, a *who,* trying to make sense of his own experience.

Thus, while the present essay may convey meanings not easily translatable into scientific propositions, perhaps it can succeed in expressing a plausible worldview within which to order some of our present-day experiences concerning the phenomena of ethnicity.

The New Ethnicity

Ethnicity is a baffling reality—morally ambivalent, paradoxical in experience, elusive in concept. World travelers observe that cultures differ from one another in mores and manners. Diplomats recognize that even the simplest gestures, words, or behaviors may signal multiple meanings. Nearly everyone recognizes that culture affects the subjectivity of individuals as well as their outward behavior. Culture shapes sensibility and perception, expectation and imagination, aspiration and moral striving, intellect and worldview. Yet it cannot be said that most highly educated persons are well prepared to account for the multicultural experiences available to them in the present age. Our theories about cultural differences and ethnic nuances are not as deep, broad, or subtle as our experience. Some philosophical distinctions may, therefore, be useful in charting this fascinating but treacherous terrain.

"Culture" is not an easy concept, since so many institutions, rituals, and practices contribute to its shaping. Its ramifications are sweeping, subtle, and often unarticulated. Its effects upon us often lie below the threshold of words or even of consciousness. The culture that has shaped us shapes our way of experiencing and perceiving, of imagining and speaking, so deeply that it is very difficult to think our way outside it. It teaches us what to regard as relevant and what to count as evidence; it provides our *canons* of relevance and evidence. We are not "products" of a culture in the way that objects are produced by a machine. Indeed, we must make conscious and voluntary efforts if we intend to appropriate our culture wholly, to go to its depths and to master its multiple possibilities. Cultures are freely elaborated by human beings; they lie, as the German philosophers were wont to say, in the realm of freedom, and the variety of human cultures on this planet is testimony to the capacities of human liberty over and above the necessities of nature. An individual passing over from his or her native culture into a culture quite different may experience "culture shock"; may, that is, come into a set of presuppositions, expectations, criteria for perception and evaluation and behavior so different as to undermine much that was previously taken for granted.

The concept of "ethnicity" has traditionally been seen as somewhat narrower than, although related to, the concept of culture. From earliest times, distinctive social groups found themselves living under the shaping influence of a common culture. In a sense, what made such social groups distinctive were the prior shaping influences of diverse cultures. Yet one could speak of a new overarching culture—Mesopotamian, Greek, Roman—within which the concept of ethnicity pointed to less all-embracing cultural influences. It is useful to note that within a concept like "Western culture," for example, quite dramatic, pervasive, and persistent sources of cultural distinctiveness have remained vital. In philosophy, to choose but one example, there are quite different creative impulses, presuppositions, methods, standards, and criteria manifested in different ethnic traditions: German, French, British, Italian, Spanish, American. In literature, theology, and in the arts it is possible simultaneously to discern characteristics that justify the notion both of a wider shared culture—Western culture—and of particular, original, and vital sources of differentiation. Humanists have not so often used the word "ethnic" to describe these differences (until recently, the word has had a ring more proper to the social sciences). From early Latin times, the tendency has rather been to speak of *nationes* (as at the University of Paris in the 12th century), not in the modern political sense but rather in a pervasive cultural sense, signifying the existence of divergent cultural entities.

It is important, then, to recognize that any humanist wishing to work out a full theory of ethnicity may find many already cherished texts in which, under other names, a tradition of giving cultural differences their due weight has been observed. Among such texts would be Alexis de Tocqueville's *Democracy in America* (1835), Ralph Waldo Emerson's *English Traits* (1856), George Santayana's *The German Mind* (originally titled *Egotism in German Philosophy*, 1939), and many others. More recent writings include Luigi Barzini's *The Italians* (1964), Jacques Maritain's *Reflections on America* (1958), and Hedrick Smith's *The Russians* (1976).

A major watershed in our thinking about ethnicity seems to have been reached in the period after World War II. As a result of the growth of international communication and of a worldwide infrastructure of technology and commerce, human beings almost everywhere have become more aware of cultures not their own. It was long imagined that the creation of "one world" would bring with it many homogenizing tendencies, based on the imperatives of universal "reason" and science and on the standardization of technological artifacts (from Coca-Cola to Shell, from transistors to computers). It was also imagined that the managers and intellectuals who operated the new international systems would create a cadre of leaders, or even perhaps a new managerial class spread around the globe, who would be almost equally at home in the urban technical environments of London, Tokyo, New York, Berlin, Rio de Janeiro, and Calcutta. The same methods, the same problems, and (roughly) the same living conditions, it was imagined, would accompany them wherever they went. Indeed, such eventualities have come to pass, largely as expected, as a result of many homogenizing influences. Political ideals—"liberation," "equality," "national sovereignty"—have crossed virtually all the world's frontiers. So have rock music and movies, jeans and automobiles.

Simultaneously, however, the late 20th century has also been marked by a resurgence of ethnic consciousness. In the Soviet Union since about 1950 the Jewish community has become increasingly conscious of its special identity and increasingly public in its self-consciousness—an attitude seen also among the ethnic Germans, Ukrainians, and other peoples of the U.S.S.R. In Great Britain, the Scots and the Welsh have demanded greater autonomy, as have the French Canadians in Canada. In Africa, Latin America, Asia, and many other places throughout the world the self-consciousness of cultural bodies has been similarly heightened. There appear to be four components of this new self-consciousness, and in examining them, it is important to pause long enough to see clearly what is new in this "new ethnicity."

The new cultural self-consciousness is, first of all, post-tribal, arising in an era in which almost every culture has been obligated to become aware of many others. In contrast to the isolation of ancient times, each culture has met at least some of the others in actual experience, and many others via the media.

Secondly, the new ethnicity arises in an era of advanced technology. This technology paradoxically liberates certain energies for more intense self-consciousness, even as it binds many cultures together in standardized technical infrastructures. The communications media, for example, are neutral with respect to cultural differences. In the techniques required to operate them and in some of their internal imperatives (scientific knowledge, technical control, precision, order) they are clearly homogenizing in effect. On the other hand, the *content* of what the media express is necessarily received by audiences affected by cultural memory, cultural differences, and distinctive cultural aspirations. Communicators who had heretofore taken their own cultural identity for granted—because it was so much a part of their daily reality that they hardly needed to be aware of it—have become more sharply aware of their own distinctive tastes, needs, and hopes in using these media. They commonly find that they must become more analytical, articulate, and self-conscious about their own distinctive voice and viewpoint.

Thirdly, the new ethnicity arises in an era of intense centripetal and homogenizing forces. Great technical power has become centered in the apparatus of the state, in the central agencies of communication, and in the central distributors of technology. These new forces call into being countervailing forces, but are themselves so powerful that a wider range of diversity can be tolerated.

These new forces also generate rebellion against "mindless" and "soulless" modernism. This rebellion represents a fourth condition for the emergence of the new ethnicity— namely, a certain discrediting of the supposed moral superiority of the modern. For some generations now, high political and moral status has accrued to all things modern, enlightened, and up to date. The forces of habit, custom, and tradition have been on the defensive. Now that the fully modern type of man or woman is everywhere more visible among us, however, the secular, pragmatic style of the proponents of modernization has lost its halo and has begun to reveal serious moral flaws. In casting about for a posture that promises a higher degree of wisdom, nobility, and relevance to ordinary people, many leaders have begun to look again at the moral sources of their traditional cultures. For most, the choice is not simply dichotomous—either traditional or modern. Rather, the status of inherited wisdom has risen, while that of the modern has slipped. In order to be evaluated, this inherited wisdom, now at last to be taken more seriously, has first to be more clearly known. Thus, the examination of "roots" has attracted both scholarly and popular attention. It is probable that a general law is here being observed: in times of moral perplexity and crisis, a reappropriation of the past, a search for renewal, gains impetus. In China there have been profound cultural cross-currents, in the United States the Bicentennial renewal, and in other cultures the drive toward cultural or national awakening; all these exhibit a strong moral dimension, fed by dissatisfaction with a merely modern morality.

In a word, peoples in every part of the world, to the surprise of those who anticipated the power only of homogen-

izing tendencies, are becoming both more aware of others
and also more aware of their own distinctive cultural identity. A heightened cultural awareness, coupled with demands for its appropriate political expression, has made of
the new ethnicity a major factor in world affairs—perhaps
even one of the major sources of political energy in our era.

Revising the Liberal Tradition

In the past, tribal consciousness was with good reason considered to be a real or potential threat to liberal and rational
institutions. While loyalty, fellow-feeling, and sympathy are
values highly prized, they are, nevertheless, moral sentiments sometimes weakened by the propensity of human
beings to limit their application to persons of their own
kind. Human beings most easily grasp through shared experience, imagination, and tacit social bonding those ways of
life most like their own. In his criticism of sentimental liberalism, *Moral Man and Immoral Society* (1932), Reinhold Nie-
buhr spelled out very clearly the limitations of such sentiments with respect to group behavior. Because of their
enduring power, however, he also distrusted such coun-
terimperatives of the modern spirit as "enlightenment" and
"rationality." These were, he thought, too optimistically set
in opposition to ties of kin, to "reasons of the blood," to inherited or ascribed status, and to related "nonrational" factors. The real world, he suggested, is more complex.

In his famous essay, "What is Enlightenment?" Immanuel
Kant singled out two elements of great importance to the
modern temper: *individuality* and *rationality*. Each individual, he argued, is an originating source of universal reason.
Each individual stands equal to every other through participation in a unifying and universally distributed rationality.
Kant locates reason, then, not in the group or social unit but
in the individual. He holds that reason is universal in its
fundamental character. In reason, persons find their individ-

uality, their unity with all other individuals, and their dignity.

It is important in the present age to defend these basic principles of enlightenment set forth, in the language of his time, by Kant and others; the declarations of fundamental human rights embraced by the United Nations depend upon such conceptions. However, it is important, as well, to recognize that the emergence of a kind of worldwide interdependence built upon a scientific and technical base, which has been achieved since the Age of Enlightenment, has also taught us much about the diversifying impact of cultural, economic, and political systems. Such systems affect the self-consciousness of individuals. They also affect the consciousness of whole social groups. No one would deny that there is a perfectly straightforward sense in which all human beings are members of the same human family; every human being is bound by imperatives of reasoning, justification, and communication across cultural and other boundaries; and each human being is entitled to claims of fundamental human dignity. Still, it is also widely grasped today that reason itself operates in pluralistic modes. It would be regarded as "cultural imperialism" to suggest that only one form of reasoning is valid in all matters. It would be regarded as naïve to believe that the content of human experiencing, imagining, understanding, judging, and deciding were everywhere the same. If anything, our age, perhaps, has learned too well the relativity of values and cultures, to the point of neglecting those things that unite all human beings as one.

It seems important for a liberal civilization today to thread its way philosophically between the Scylla of relativity and the Charybdis of too narrow a conception of universal reason. Bernard Lonergan in *Insight: A Study of Human Understanding* (1957) has suggested that it is of intellectual benefit to call attention to the difference between invariant human *operations* and the varying *content* upon which those operations work. In this way, he proposes to defend at one and the same time both the spiritual unity of the human race and that multiplicity of cultures that springs from human liberty. Unlike other animals, the human being elaborates across space and time multiple forms of behaviors and practices. Cultural differentiation is a primary characteristic of human life, a direct expression of human liberty. As a source of originating agency, possessing a capacity to perceive, to intend, and to act in a self-directed manner, each individual human person stands in a certain sense alone. Yet in living in social units, in elaborating social institutions of great complexity, each individual human being is also a social creature. As a bodily organism, each is born, suffers, is hungry, loves, dies. Yet in various cultures these fundamental identities acquire distinctive symbolic meanings. On several levels of life, individual and social, intellectual and physical, certain invariant structures of experience cut across all cultures and unite all human beings in certain specific human perplexities. Daniel Bell has theorized in *The Cultural Contradictions of Capitalism* (1976) and in his Hobhouse Lecture at the London School of Economics (1977) that cultural systems are variant solutions to fundamental and common human perplexities such as birth, suffering, love, moral consciousness, and death.

In addition, according to Lonergan, certain invariant operations of human understanding also occur across cultures: every human being experiences, imagines, understands (both in flashes of insight and in conceptual expression), judges, decides. Moreover, these operations lead to one another, and depend upon one another, in certain invariant ways. Experiences raise questions for imagination. In the dark, one feels a presence and hears a sound; is it a mosquito, the effect of anxiety, or sheer restlessness? Examples posited in imagination raise questions for understanding. (What is it?) Hypotheses conceptualized for understanding raise questions for judgment. (Is that so?) Judgments about what really is so raise questions for action. (What ought I to do?) In every culture, by every human being, such operations as these are performed daily. The manner in which they are performed, the imaginative, linguistic, and conceptual equipment with which they are performed, and the content upon which they are performed vary widely. The importance attached to one or the other of these operations also varies in different cultures. The point is that we are not entirely helpless when we attempt to find our way through the disparate cultural materials we encounter in trying to understand our shared humanity. The great intellectual work of reconciling our unity to our diversity is under way. Thus, even if we have not as yet achieved adequate methods for transcultural communication and analysis; even if our present methods of trying to order the staggering cultural variety to be found upon this globe remain at a primitive level; even if international scholarship, except perhaps in elementary scientific and technical areas, remains upon deplorably parochial and ethnocentric bases—despite all this, the task of developing a truly international intellectual perspective is not in principle beyond us.

Thus, the enterprise of constructing, as it were, a new form of "universal reason" remains yet to be accomplished. It remains a valid aim for enlightened and liberal scholarship. To be sure, the discovery by each of the world's cultures of the almost immediate presence of the others has come upon the world rather suddenly, with the advent of instant communications and rapid travel since World War II. Admittedly, too, naïve and simple forms of rationality, and even the supposition that the liberal spirit itself is to be understood in one way only, have had to be modified under the pressure of the discovery of immense human variety. Still, individual human beings have been able to perform truly remarkable acts of understanding concerning cultures not their own. There is no reason to believe that the number of such explorers and interpreters will not grow.

If there was a temptation for the rationalist wing of the liberal movement (represented by Kant) to suppose a simpler and more immediate path to "universal reason" than has proved to be possible, that is no justification for refusing to embrace the possibilities of a more cosmopolitan form of the liberal spirit. If there was a temptation for the romantic wing of Western culture (Nietzsche may serve as an example) to exalt differences at the expense of the intellectual enterprise of human unity, that is no reason for conceding to despair. Different materials may be understood differently, in more than one way, by more than one method. Reasoning by way of analogy is possible. One may "cross over" from one mode of cultural experience into another, with remarkable gains in mutual understanding. It is not necessary to reduce one culture to the terms of another, invidiously or even imperialistically, in order to penetrate some, at least, of the secrets of its way of life. The way of understanding is never without trial and error. Where some explorers fail, others may do better. The enterprise of intellectual understanding and cultural sympathy stands upon firm ground and is not undercut by repeated failures.

It is a mistake, then, to hold that the new ethnic consciousness is necessarily a counterrational or illiberal force. So long as the commitment to the intellectual enterprise of mutual understanding remains firm, the new cultural consciousness need not collapse into ethnic chauvinism. Insofar as the new ethnic consciousness may prove to be a post-tribal development, it would be tragic to permit it to be reduced to merely tribal intelligence. In those cases, indeed, where that reduction has taken place, the consequences are amply displayed for everyone's contempt. Indeed, the contempt we feel on such occasions is a sign that such reductionism, far from being necessary, evinces a radical human failure.

The new liberal spirit, I propose, should rest upon two pillars: a firm commitment to the laborious but rewarding enterprise of full, mutual, intellectual understanding; and a respect for differences of nuance and subtlety, particularly in the area of those diversifying "lived values" that have lain until now, in all cultures, so largely unarticulated. In this sense, the true liberal spirit is *cosmopolitan* rather than *universalist*. The connotations of those two words suggest the difference between a liberalism that expects, and desires, a certain homogenization and a liberalism that expects, and delights in, variety. Cosmopolitan liberalism is surely closer to the heart of the authentic liberal spirit. Just as Kant was eager to defend the uniqueness of individuals (despite his tendency to imagine universal and general laws), so cosmopolitan liberalism is eager to respect the individuality of cultures.

The Pluralistic Personality

Culture is not only external to the individual. The individual interiorizes, appropriates, and carries culture. A culture has vitality only if it lives in the skills, disciplines, morals, and manners of individuals, only if it is carried even in the motions of the individual heart. Individuals continually re-create, modify, and enrich cultures.

In a pluralistic nation like the United States, cultural diversity plays a unique psychological role. Indeed, it appears to be bringing about the development of a unique psychological type: the pluralistic personality. Although many scores of different groups may be distinguished among the American people (the number varies with the criteria employed) this nation may not be the most linguistically and culturally diverse of nations. It is possible that the peoples of the U.S.S.R., India, China, Brazil, Canada, and other nations are at least as pluralistic as are our own. Yet, from a very early period, American society was established upon three significant principles which have led to a unique experiment in pluralistic living. These three principles have provided an important measure of a civilized reconciliation of unity and diversity, for the inspection of other nations and for any future world civilization.

First, in the United States, ethnicity has not been permitted to become an instrument of territorial sovereignty, or of political exclusion in any jurisdiction. It is not permitted to become the exclusive instrument of political organization. Political rights inhere in individuals, not in ethnic groups.

Second, individuals are free to make as much, or as little, of their ethnic belonging as they choose. No one is to be coerced into a system of ethnic identification he does not choose for himself.

Third, individuals organized together in voluntary associations are encouraged to nourish such sentiments, memories, aspirations, and practices of group life as they choose. In such matters, the state is not only neutral but positively encouraging, through favorable tax laws and other legal principles. The social dimensions of individual life are thereby recognized.

It is considered something of a sin against "the American way" for persons to be made to feel that they *must* be identified by social characteristics; for the law so to distinguish them; or for individual social groups to coerce their members into such identification. Many rituals and practices have been established, from public ceremonies of representation to such political practices as the "balanced ticket," whose purpose is symbolically to include every group of Americans within the public presence of "the American people," and to strengthen in each breast the sentiment, "We are all Americans now." In this sense, the "melting pot" has been a powerful myth and an effective practice in American life. The concept of the American people is designed to include all equally, without discrimination. On the other hand, the oath of citizenship does not require any individual to renounce his or her former cultural belonging or cultural history. In order to become a U.S. citizen, one does not have to cease living from and being nourished by the cultural traditions of one's native inheritance. In this sense, "the melting pot" does not entail the melting away of cultural differences among the American people.

The result of this special experiment in pluralism is that

many Americans develop what might be called a "pluralistic personality." Each individual is, by right and by opportunity, responsible for choosing his or her own identity from among the many materials presented by the contingencies of human life. In a society like ours, an individual participates in the cultural life of more than one social group. We are each differentiated by such characteristics as age, sex, religion, biological and cultural inheritance, marriage, education, occupation, region, locality, personal exploration, and voluntary association. In at least such senses, everybody (or virtually everybody) participates in more than one social group and carries multiple associational identities. One person may be, for example, a New Yorker by birth, a professional humanist, a liberal in politics, Jewish, of parents who emigrated from eastern Europe, and by choice chiefly interested in associations and projects that establish his identity as future-oriented and assimilationist. Of some of these forms of "belonging," the individual in question may choose to make little or nothing, to pursue, as it were, a form of forgetfulness; while on others the individual may choose to focus his energy fully. Another individual of similar background might make a quite different choice.

Notwithstanding an individual's conscious choices, however, each person is also influenced by social factors over which he or she has had no control. We do not choose our grandparents, nor the basic lines of our early nurture. We do not choose (entirely) how others will regard us or what, even despite our best intentions, they may ascribe to us. Moreover, even the patterns of our conscious choices—our careers, successes, living patterns, educational choices, political behaviors, and incomes—may be studied by those who quantify our age, sex, religion, ethnicity, or other group-shared characteristics. Even if we do not choose to be "ethnic," in other words, even if we consciously renounce or disregard our cultural inheritance, it can hardly surprise us that sociologists or other students of social life will notice, at least in a generalized way, materials of ethnic specificity in our outward behavior. Finally, our own conscious choices with respect to our own cultural belonging may change over time, both in extension and in intensity. Personal experiences, or changes in the world around us (the precariousness of the state of Israel, for example, or turmoil in Ireland) may conspire to alter in us our own sense of identity.

"Ethnic belonging," then, is a phenomenon of human consciousness and is subject to multiple influences and multiple transformations, in ourselves and in the eyes of others. Its importance for any individual or group may change over time. Ethnicity is not a simple phenomenon; it is not easy to define in terms that apply in precisely the same way to everyone.

In a pluralistic society like that of the United States, moreover, many persons have the opportunity to become involved in many cultural traditions not originally their own, and to appropriate music, ideas, values, and even a set of intellectual landmarks not native to their own upbringing. We find that each of us can live from many diverse spiritual sources. In this respect, too, ecumenical and multicultural activities nourish in us a pluralistic personality—a personality rooted in multiple sources of spiritual power.

In the American system, then, the ideal of ethnic belonging has a special quality. It includes not only a willingness to cooperate democratically with those nourished by other traditions, but also an openness toward learning from others. It includes a willingness to appropriate from other traditions admirable traits and purposes, and fruitful sources of insight and sensibility. The notion of a wholly closed form of ethnic belonging—entirely inward-turning and wholly resistant to others—has come to seem seriously flawed. Even those within various traditions who propose the strengthening and deepening of their own cultural traditions normally find themselves working closely with others outside their own cultural group. They feel quite honored to be cited for their services to other communities or to the nation as a whole. Thus, American life provides many inhibitions against "tribalism," both within individual groups and within the culture as a whole. Indeed, the normal worry is that homogenizing and simply ecumenical influences are, if anything, out of balance, and threaten to overwhelm the influences of differentiation and cultural continuity.

As a result, individuals in our society tend to develop a plurality of cultural roots. Those of us who are not by ancestry Anglo-American learn to assimilate the values, attitudes, and practices of—as it seems to us—one of the most liberating of the world's traditions. We gladly learn its political history, its language, and its literature. From Jewish traditions, we learn both a psychiatric and sociological sophistication, a way of looking beneath the surface of the self and of society, and a sense of the long reality of Western history as it was experienced by Jews. From black culture, Indian culture, from the multiple Catholic cultures, from the cultures of Asia and of Latin America we appropriate other cherished values.

In the sense that all citizens share major national experiences—prosperity and depression, war and peace, great moral leadership, sad official lapses, and the assassinations of beloved figures—all of us participate in a "common culture." This common culture is built up, as well, by the tacit and powerful influences of a common language and the experience of common legal, economic, and political traditions. Yet the many cultures so united are vast, rich, and various, so that individuals do not assimilate all of them equally. In this sense, each individual lives, as well, from the particular cultures in which he or she was born and reared, and from which it has been his or her good fortune or free choice to learn. Thus, we each forge our own individual cultural identity, drawing (almost always) upon more than one tradition. In this sense, too, we each develop "a pluralistic personality," and are individually able to understand implicitly and to dwell with tacit ease in more than one cultural tradition.

A complicating factor in the attempt to sort out the many strands of actual American life as it is experienced from many standpoints—by a Filipino in Hawaii, a Polish American in Los Angeles, a Chicano in Chicago, a Georgia Baptist at Yale, a North Carolina black in New York—is the relative silence of the public media and of public discourse generally about these multiple differences. It is, perhaps, impossible to have a public language, especially for expression through media whose scope is national, which is simultaneously understandable by all and fully expressive of the nation's variety. Public communications are necessarily pitched to a kind of lowest common denominator. They reflect no specific subculture fully. In this sense, a public sort of "superculture" is imposed upon the top of the many subcultures of the land. Nearly everybody learns this national argot, which is in large measure commercial in its purposes and its utility.

"Superculture" is not precisely the same concept as "mass culture." For those forms of communication that are aimed at the national "high culture," the shared culture of national elites, are also conducted within it. The reporter or the commentator who speaks through the national media of communication is expected to exhibit a form of sophistication that is higher than that of "mass culture." In this sense, "superculture" is guarded by its own elite. But both superculture and mass culture aim at a level that is above the nation's pluralism. In order to develop a theory about the relations between the shared common culture of the American people and the particular cultural streams from which individuals draw their nourishment, it is necessary to notice how superculture and mass culture overlay, rather than grow out of, the many particular cultures that constitute our people. These overlays are probably indispensable to our system of national communication. They generate a form of ersatz culture, a sort of false consciousness, insofar as they arise from no particular culture but are constructed for broad communication.

A sign of this artificiality becomes apparent when one notices how many television shows—but also weighty generalizations about our national life and national character—actually represent no one neighborhood, no single culture or region, but appear rather to represent a fictional "nowhere," a construct designed on some superficial level to represent almost everyone. It is virtually impossible to refer accurately and profoundly to everyone at once, and so this flaw in our national self-understanding is no doubt inevitable. But it does require continuous intellectual correction. When one hears sentences about "middle Americans," or "typical American values," it is usually instructive to try to visualize the actual and complex variety that such sentences attempt to cover. Such reflection often brings to one's attention materials of considerable political and moral significance. Our variety confounds our need for easy generalizations.

In self-defense, then, those who try to retain their grip on reality develop techniques of translation. We each, privately and implicitly, learn to read between the lines of public speech and to focus upon concrete realities dear to us. In this way, we often mentally cross over from one cultural horizon to another. Some, for example, inspect public generalizations for their accuracy concerning blacks, or women, or specific ethnic groups. This capacity for accepting the common idiom, while mentally translating it into one's own horizon, illustrates the pluralistic personality at work.

The pluralistic personality has, then, a quite unique historical range and liberty. Such a personality, for all its broad experience and liberty of action, is not "rootless." Under the conditions of the old ethnicity, the consciousness of many may have been essentially parochial and isolated. Under the conditions of the new ethnicity, a capacity to enter into multiple perspectives, and to see the same matter from more than one point of view seems to represent a clear gain for the human spirit. Without depending upon a kind of universal homogenization, it represents an admirable development in the liberal spirit, and a new type of social personality in human history. It is produced almost effortlessly by the sort of institutional life our pluralistic society has developed. Naturally, some individuals represent the pluralistic personality in fuller development, others in lesser. Every human being suffers from some degree of limited sympathy and limited perception. No one can claim to have a godlike capacity to understand everything about everything. The pluralistic personality discovers that learning comes by way of a certain humility, a certain hesitance to judge others too quickly, a certain generous watchfulness for possible errors in his own perceptions.

Ethnicity and the Soul

Such humility is necessary because the ways by which ethnic heritage affects an individual's inner life are subtle and complex, and mistakes of interpretation are easy. In the United States persons of Anglo-American stock have found their own heritage reinforced by the common use of English, continued close ties to the culture of Great Britain, the study of English literature, and the continuity of many institutional forms in politics and law. Those who stand directly in the line of these major cultural institutions may not be especially aware of their own cultural tradition; it forms so immediate a part of their daily reality that it may seem to them like second nature. Those Americans whose native traditions are not Anglo-American have had, by contrast, to adapt to new institutional and cultural forms, to learn not only a new language but also a new repertoire of gestures, mores, and manners. More deeply than that, many have had to learn new ways of thinking, feeling, and imagining. Great energy was expended in the process of assimilating this rich and liberating culture. In response, America itself changed under the impact of mass immigration. The common culture was altered by being assimilated in fresh ways. Even descendants of British Americans have had to adapt to a new common culture not identical to their own. Our common culture, then, belongs to no one ethnic group, although much of it has an Anglo-American origin, and it simultaneously allows diversity to thrive, less so in national public speech but more so in living communities of thought and feeling.

Measures of external behavior then—in education, politics, occupation, income, and other areas—continue to reflect differences among individuals that are related to their cultures of origin. The social scientists note these differences well enough, but the most neglected and unexplored dimension of ethnicity lies in the fields of the humanities: how ethnicity affects the individual spirit, in its tastes, memories, aspirations, and systems of value and meaning.

There are some major intellectual difficulties blocking the way to the humanistic analysis of such materials. It is useful to mention these first. The humanistic tradition wishes, first of all, to defend the individual. Hence, one cluster of difficulties surrounds the dangers of stereotyping. Each culture, in its institutions, its religions, and its literature, celebrates a distinctive constellation of human values and upholds a distinctive set of cultural heroes, saints, and everyday models. The ideals of the French intellectual, for example, are not identical to those of the British. The folk heroes of various cultures differ; children's stories celebrate diverse values or styles. Reasons of climate or political history may have brought about the celebration of differentiated human qualities necessary for a group's survival or historical advance. The role of great originating geniuses early in the history of a culture—King Arthur, say—may have attracted the love and imitation of millions through the ages. Music, folk arts, drama, dance, games, the liturgies of church and the state, the sermonic or rhetorical forms of public discourse, and other elements of this sort may continuously have promoted certain forms of behavior and discouraged others. The arts of storytelling may have inculcated narrative expectations that celebrated cleverness, bold action, humility, creative arrogance, wit, endurance, obedience, fidelity, and so on. Finally, the economic or social order of a culture may have inculcated modes of realism—enterprise and openness, say, as opposed to a passion for security—different from those inculcated in a different economic or social system. In all these ways, culture differs from culture. In a kind of shorthand, world travelers or students of comparative culture develop brief, often anecdotal descriptions that attempt to capture the distinctive aspects of each culture. One speaks —to reduce the shorthand to adjectival dimensions—of the "phlegmatic" English, the "orderly" Germans, the "romantic" Latins, the "hotblooded" Spaniards, the "stubborn" Poles, the "melancholy" Danes, and the like. The danger of stereotyping is great.

In this respect, there is a critical difference between generalizations employed about the distinctive characteristics of cultures and scientific descriptions. Scientific descriptions formulate laws based on individual behaviors. Cultures do not exercise so total a control over individuals; hence, cultural effects cannot be reduced to such descriptions. Cultures do establish distinctive ideals and perhaps even distinctive catalogues of especially abhorred sins. These then exert a kind of attraction and repulsion upon individuals born within a culture. Those who reveal in their own behavior a kind of fulfillment of the highest ideals of the culture are normally singled out for special praise and rewards, and those who do not measure up are, accordingly, less rewarded.

Generalizations about cultural characteristics must, further, observe four other conditions. First, in most complex cultures more than one set of cultural ideals is available; second, cultures are normally open to change, so that new types of cultural heroes regularly emerge; third, the function of cultural ideals is not to describe all members of a society but rather to single out, to promote, and to reward certain forms of behavior; fourth, each individual appropriates the ideals of a culture in a free and distinctive way, sometimes by rebelling against them, resisting them, muting them, or playing counterpoint against them. Without denying the force of distinctive cultural ideals upon the whole everyday life of cultures, it is important to see the wide range of liberty still exercised by individuals within them. It is a mistake to apply to individuals the generalizations that attempt to define the working ideals of a culture; this mistake is properly called stereotyping.

Nonetheless, the power of the distinctive ideals of a culture, together with the mores and manners that support them, makes entrance into a new culture difficult for refugees, emigrants, or others who move from one culture to another. The prospect of exile may hold an understandable dread for fully formed adults; they may doubt their capacity to adapt, and they may fear psychological isolation when the outer conditions of their new world will no longer supply the daily signals that they internalized as children within a different culture. On the other hand, migrants sometimes experience a release in the new culture, which rewards in them qualities of mind, heart, or action that may have been repressed in their culture of origin. Thus does the impact of a culture upon an individual affect the entire soul: every instinct, emotional response, imagination, perception, sensibility, habit of mind. "Assimilation" is often spoken of too lightly.

Generalizations about a culture are dangerous in another way. Many of the ideals or tendencies within a culture are all the more powerful for being tacit. They are most often expressed in practice not as maxims to be memorized, or as codes clearly written out. They emerge, rather, from the tacit distribution of inhibitions and rewards built into institutions, practices, and mores. To put such inhibitions into sentences is often to falsify them. Thus, for example, one may say that Americans are taught to be acquisitive. Putting matters this way, one seems to be indicting Americans for conscious and articulated motives, which many might deny holding, whereas the generalization might merely have been pointing to the unparalleled abundance of unused and unneeded things which many Americans seem to accumulate around them. Yet Jacques Maritain noted in *Reflections on America* that the imputed "materialism" of the American character, an accusation made not only by foreigners but by many Americans as well, actually represents in practice a most remarkable indifference to material things, which because so abundant are held cheap in the calculus of human purposes. In the same way, generalizations about other cultures must be examined with great care.

To put the matter in another way, such generalizations frequently make conscious materials that were in practice unconscious. When such generalizations are carefully formed, they may by that very fact seem to go beyond the materials they point to. The well-established but tacit practices they describe no longer seem to be the same when codified in propositions, for such practices do not function as conscious moral rules, ideals, or approved courses of action. Many aspects of manners, mores, and even morals, once examined and raised before consciousness in propositional form, may come into conflict with other values in the culture. Cultures are such complicated systems of multiple imperatives that they contain many internal conflicts, which are normally resolved only over long stretches of time.

Finally, it must be noted that many aspects of cultural life, just because they have been internalized in tacit and unconscious ways, are difficult to discern in one's own life. It is hard to step outside one's own culture, so as to see it whole. Even when made conscious, aspects of culture such as the distinctively American attitude toward law, for example, are often difficult to articulate in words. It is one of the functions of literature to hold up a mirror to culture in which such secrets of the inner life may be reflected, not by abstraction, but in the full concrete texture of the represented situation. Literature succeeds as an instrument of understanding, where scientific description may fail, by rendering the lived forms of life in anecdotal segments so that tacit understandings and practices may be rendered for inspection through a method different from that of abstraction.

In American life, correspondingly, both literary materials and methods of "participant observation," as employed in sociology, anthropology, and journalism, are among our best sources for understanding the impact of ethnicity upon our inner lives. Irving Howe's remarkable study *World of Our Fathers* (1976), Michael Arlen's *Passage to Ararat* (1975), Richard Gambino's *Blood of My Blood* (1974), Alex Haley's *Roots* (1976), John Gregory Dunne's *True Confessions* (1977), and many other books reveal the quite different instincts, attitudes, aspirations, and perceptions that actually motivate diverse individuals in our midst.

Ethnic identity persists among individuals, it appears, by being passed on in unconscious, tacit ways in their early nurture. The laws of such transmission are not well understood. It appears that in some families the mother and in others the father—perhaps sometimes in different respects —pass on some of the values and expectations that he or she internalized from the long line of human tradition. More study of such matters would no doubt be rewarding, for it is certain that individuals do not spring like Venus from the sea, but are social beings. The attractions and inhibitions acquired by the workings of cultures upon history are passed on through individuals. No one of us represents all the cultures of humanity, yet each of us carries social meanings and values not invented by ourselves. The reason for studying such sociality in our individual makeup is not to promote "ethnic pride," for not all that we carry forward is wholly admirable. The primary reason is to obtain self-knowledge.

Normally, our experience with central elements of culture —with a concept of God, for example—is highly colored by the culture passed on to us by our parents. Scholars do not take for granted that the images of God, and the complex of attitudes deemed appropriate for approaching God, are exactly the same in every culture, even of those which are generically Christian. Rather, in different cultures, systems of worship and liturgy, of preaching and of practice, subtly build up quite distinctive languages of the soul. In some cultures, religion is more closely identified with morality, in such a way that God is imagined rather like a great seeing eye of conscience (the "objective observer" of some Anglo-American philosophical theories, for example). In other cultures, particularly in southern and eastern Europe, religion is more closely identified with nature, in such a way that God is imagined rather as the source of unity in all things. In the former, a person who is religious but not moral may be regarded as "not really religious." In the latter, there is a distance between being religious and being moral, such that even a person who is quite moral may not be perceived as religious, and even a person of less than admirable moral practice may yet be perceived as quite religious. In some cultures history, and in other cultures nature, provides the psychological dynamism of religion. In some the individual, and in others the family or the local community, is the basic unit from which moral values are derived. Similarly, in tacit conceptions of authority and dissent, of masculinity and femininity, of social loyalty and individually defined moral principle, culture differs from culture.

The "voice" and "temperature" of cultures in the home appear also to be communicated from generation to generation to the psyches of children. The constellations within which the various passions and modes of intelligence are distributed appear to vary from culture to culture. Expression of an emotion like anger may be inhibited in some cultures, and regarded as a failure in self-control; in others, anger may be a quite familiar and uninhibited passion. Orderliness may be given high value in some cultures, and low value in others.

How often children are held in the arms, by whom, and in which emotional patterns may establish the rhythm of their own future emotional expectations. How many voices surround them and with what qualities of passion, what is encouraged in their behavior and what is inhibited, the repertoire of facial expression and gesture and information that they absorb—all these are communicated, most often, without theory and apart from conscious decision. So it goes also for the rudiments of religious, political, sexual, and other attitudes. Expectations are established, tonalities become familiar, schemes of approval and disapproval are internalized, emotions are given shape, perceptions are tutored, evil and good are identified.

The history of these transmissions from generation to generation does reflect some change and alteration within cultures, but not much. Almost always, usually through signals below the threshold of consciousness, generation leaps across generation in cultural continuity. Even in rebellion, the sons pass on more of their fathers than they know, the daughters of their mothers. Sometimes, in generation-skipping sequences, the life of the grandfather seems to be recapitulated more in that of the grandson than of the son. Because of a long emphasis on the rational and the individual, scholars have done too little work on the patterns of transmitting culture through the generations and on the general theme of cultural continuity.

There are certain central symbolic clusters in personal life in which cultural traditions tend to be concentrated. Even in persons not aware of their own cultural indebtedness, one often finds in the patterns of their tastes, orientations, values, and repugnances clear signals from the past. Imagination and sensibility are especially affected by family culture, but so also is the pattern of perception, the way intelligence works, and desire and aspiration. One cannot understand the dramatic success of individuals who are Jewish, both in the schools and in the world of enterprise, without understanding as well the specific strengths of the culture that nourished them both in eastern Europe and in the United States. This is particularly striking when one compares the trajectory of the individual lives of eastern European Jewish immigrants with that of those whose ancestors also came from eastern Europe, at about the same time, but who were not Jewish; or with that of other cultural groups.

Among the nodal points for cross-cultural comparison, one could single out at least eight that could illuminate a wide spectrum of other attitudes and behavior: attitudes toward the divine, the sacred, or the holy; attitudes toward nature, history, and moral striving; attitudes toward intelligence, learning, and ideas; attitudes toward the rein to be given passion and emotion, and in which respects; attitudes toward authority, the past, tradition; attitudes toward the individuality or the communality of human living, toward solitude and solidarity, self and family; attitudes toward masculinity and fathering, toward femininity and mothering; attitudes toward the power of goodness and the power of evil in human affairs. Cultures, like individuals, differ remarkably from one another in such matters. One might turn to rites of passage, to sports, to ceremonies of birth and marriage and death, and to other locations in each culture for clues as to how the above-mentioned attitudes are passed on to new generations. There are many methods for studying such attitudes. In many families, attention has for some generations now been drawn to what is "new" and "American" in the experience of individuals, rather than to what is continuous with cultures of the past. That imbalance might now be corrected.

If each of us takes a moment to reflect upon our own deepest associations with such symbols as those mentioned above, we cannot help encountering our radical and fundamental debt to the generations that have preceded us. To be sure, we are free to turn in new directions, to erase or at least to cover over the tracings of the past. We are not imprisoned by our social and cultural inheritance, but we have, in fact, felt its imprint and have been given at least nascent definition by it. Until recently, Americans have not often made explicit connection to their cultural heritage or heritages. To have done so would have been to fly in the face of the strong emphasis in American life upon the principle that we are all individuals, responsible for re-creating ourselves anew. This principle conveys a great and important truth: each of us is responsible for creating his or her own identity. But a companion principle also conveys an important truth: each of us is a social creature, in part shaped by the others of whom we are a part; our destiny is familial as well as individual.

Discussions about values and meaning often go astray in America because the concrete contexts that give flesh and blood to our individual experience of life are left out of account. The eight symbolic clusters mentioned above focus the attention of specific cultures in diverse ways, lead each to interpret the same data within a different horizon of meaning and value, and inculcate in each different sources of attraction and repulsion. Different traditions instruct individuals differently in what power they possess to change things. In some, the tragic sense is strong, or cultural pessimism, or patience; in others, idealism and hope are very bright. The differences among us as individuals are often accounted for by phrases such as "to each his own," as though our ethical visions and choices came strictly through individual choice. Actually, it appears, there is in each individual a considerably larger range of cultural principles at work than we seem to notice. Patterns emerge. Traditions come into focus. We are not so independent or so idiosyncratic as we have been led to imagine. There is a general descriptive geography to our moral visions and choices. A kind of general "field theory" of moral symbols powerful among Americans might be developed. Anglo-American, Jewish, black, Italian, and other ethnic cultures have established significant magnetic lodes in this field, which exert contrasting forces upon large numbers of individuals.

The full cultural history of American religion has yet to be written. Accurate and detailed attention to its component historical cultures is still in its infancy. The multicultural materials of American literary history have yet to be fully explored. Particularly interesting are the ways in which a writer in one cultural tradition—a Jewish novelist, say— perceives in his work the secret springs of those who are of a different tradition. In these matters, the way people perceive each other is a valid and important subject of study.

The many divergent ways in which central cultural symbols actually function in the daily lives of Americans have not yet been mapped. The ways in which ethnicity has affected, and still does affect, the inner lives of Americans have not yet been fully explored. One hopes that in religion, philosophy, and literature, as well as in psychology and the social sciences, the materials for such a study will be assembled, and that by the time another generation passes the state of our knowlege will be considerably more concrete and exact than it is at present.

3
AMERICAN IDENTITY AND AMERICANIZATION

The term "identity" has become indispensable in the discussion of ethnic affairs. Yet it was hardly used at all until the 1950s. The father of the concept, Erik H. Erikson, remarked on its novelty in his widely read book *Childhood and Society* (1950): "We begin to conceptualize matters of identity at the very time in history when they become a problem. For we do so in a country which attempts to make a superidentity out of all the identities imported by its constituent immigrants." In an autobiographical account published 20 years later, Erikson, himself an immigrant, quoted this passage and added that the terms "identity" and "identity crisis" seemed to grow out of "the experience of emigration, immigration, and Americanization."

The relationship between ethnicity and American identity —or super-identity, as Erikson called it—is complex and elusive. The difficulty of talking about it is compounded because the terms we must use are inescapably multivalent and can be understood in many different senses. For this reason, it is desirable to be as explicit as possible about the terms at the outset.

First, "American identity" will be employed here interchangeably with "American nationality" and "American character." It is true that these are vague expressions, and that distinctions could be introduced among them, but their imprecision accurately reflects the indeterminacy of the phenomena to which they refer, and in common usage these expressions are more or less synonymous. Even Erikson, whose definition of psychological identity is highly specific, writes as though national identity and national character were pretty much the same thing. It should also be noted that "identity" as used here is not intended to convey specifically Eriksonian psychological connotations but is to be understood in a looser, more informal sense.

Second, the aim of this essay is the relatively modest one of reviewing historically the place of ethnicity in the tradition of thinking and writing about American identity. My intention, in other words, is not to establish what the relationship of ethnicity to American identity actually is or was, but to ascertain the relative *salience* that issues we now think of as ethnic have had when Americans have debated among themselves about what it means to be an American.

The Ideological Origins of American Identity (1776–1815)

Although there were glimmerings of a sense of American distinctiveness in the late colonial period, it was the separation of the colonies from Great Britain by the Declaration of Independence and the Revolution that created the need for a national consciousness as the spiritual counterpart of the political entity that had come into being. The revolutionary generation was quite cognizant of the fact that nation building required not just fashioning viable political institutions but also nurturing an American nationality in keeping with the values, philosophy, and outlook embodied in the Constitution and the laws. The fact that the American people were of diverse ethnic strains was not overlooked in discussions of nationality, but because of the nature of the events that brought the nation to birth, the American identity was conceived primarily in abstract ideological terms. Ethnic considerations were subsidiary.

More than two decades ago, Hans Kohn emphasized the ideological nature of American nationalism. A sense of distinctive peoplehood could be founded only on ideas, he pointed out, because the great majority of Americans shared language, literature, religion, and other cultural traditions with the nation against which they had successfully rebelled and from which they were most determined to establish their spiritual as well as political independence. The non-British minority did not offer a language, religion, or common culture upon which the national identity could be based. The foundation of nationality had to be laid on the same bedrock of political principle that justified separation from the mother country and underlay the constitutional framework. The United States defined itself as a nation by commitment to the principles of liberty, equality, and government on the basis of consent, and the nationality of its people derived from their identification with those principles.

Two elements can be distinguished in the structure of ideas underlying American national identity. First, there was the English tradition of liberty that stressed self-government, institutional limitations on the power of the sovereign, and procedural safeguards in law for the person accused of a crime. The earliest protests against the imperial policies of the British in the 1760s appealed to this tradition, for although the rights of Englishmen were prescriptive and not doctrinaire, the American colonists considered themselves participants in the tradition and entitled by birthright to the privileges and protection that were their heritage. Only when Parliament and the king rejected their interpretation of the traditional rights of Englishmen did Americans turn to a second, more abstract and theoretical line of argument. Here they were able to draw upon the thinkers of the Enlightenment, who had been inspired by the example of English liberties but who had transformed those lessons into universal principles. Thus, as Kohn puts it, "The historical birthright of Englishmen became in America, under the influence of eighteenth-century ideas, the natural right of man, a universal message, the birthright of mankind." Each of these elements was necessary. If it had not been rooted in the empirical English institutional and procedural tradition, American liberty might have destroyed itself in utopian extremism, but without the additional dimension of Enlightenment universalism, America could not have become the "asylum of liberty" for all people, regardless of national origin.

This formulation requires some modification today in the light of the work done on republican ideology. As a number of scholars have shown, the American patriots drew heavily on a tradition of British political writing that went back to the middle of the 17th century and linked there with classical republican thought, which had been revived in the Renaissance, particularly in Machiavelli's *Discourses* on Livy's history of Rome. This scholarship suggests that the theoretical dimension of American ideology is less dependent on the continental writers of the 18th century than Kohn believed. However, it does not shake his central insight that American nationality rests on a structure of ideas about freedom, equality, and self-government and that this ideology combines abstract, universalist elements with a historically grounded appreciation of the practical machinery for self-government and protection of individual liberties.

Besides uncovering different sources for revolutionary political ideas, scholars of the republican school have shown that these ideas carried the deepest kind of moral significance. A republic demanded virtue of its citizens, for only a people willing to subordinate private gain to the good of the polity could govern itself. The citizenry must be vigilant in guarding against corruption in its rulers and in the community at large. Simplicity and self-reliance were the most effectual guarantees, for the former preserved the people from the enervating effects of luxury, and the latter removed them from dependence on the good will and largess of others, which made them subject to corruption. The "cultivators of the earth" lovingly described by Jefferson in his *Notes on Virginia* were God's chosen people precisely because the life of the yeoman farmer accorded so well with the prescriptions of simplicity, self-reliance, and virtue imposed by the republican ideology.

Jefferson believed that the safety of the American republic was secure so long as the nation was composed primarily of independent yeoman farmers, but he trembled at the prospect that the servile masses of Europe might overwhelm the nation by immigration. Others used the republican ideology to argue in favor of building up commerce and manufacturing, even if that required inducing skilled European mechanics to emigrate to the United States. How could the nation remain self-reliant and virtuous if it was completely dependent upon other states for its manufactured goods? Thus republicanism did not provide unambiguous guidelines to policy, and it was not without competing theories about the relation between private behavior and civic well-being. The rising current of utilitarian thought was based on the assumption that there was such a thing as legitimate self-love, that actions dictated by self-interest might be perfectly compatible with general social benefit, and that civic virtue did not always require Spartan self-denial.

Insofar as republicanism was an element in the ideological basis of American identity, it added to the moral intensity and precariousness of the American experiment. The republican emphasis on virtue invested politics with religious seriousness and encouraged men to look upon policy disagreements as the reflection of fundamental qualities of good or evil in personal character. This line of thinking, which blended easily with what has been called "civil millennialism," helps explain why the 1790s were a period of superheated controversy, in which partisanship reached levels of utter frenzy, and charges of treason, corruption, and moral depravity became staples of political discourse. Because it made the success of republican government contingent upon an almost heroic kind of disinterestedness and civic vigilance, the republican ideology added to the difficulties of establishing a political order that would realize in practice the high principles proclaimed as the foundation of national existence.

But the very precariousness of their experiment made Americans highly self-conscious about their national identity. One could collect many references to the national character, from Thomas Paine's plea in 1783 for unity among the states as a basis for American nationality to Henry Clay's remark in 1815 that the just-concluded war with England had achieved one of its principal objects, "the firm establishment of the national character." Erik Erikson expressed the surprise modern readers feel on encountering this degree of self-consciousness: "It is hard for us to believe . . . how conscious these early Americans were of the job of developing American character out of the regional and generational polarities and contradictions of a nation of immigrants and migrants." Three marks of the developing idea of nationality are especially significant.

First, the ideological quality of American national identity was of decisive importance vis-à-vis the question of immigration and ethnicity. To be or to become an American, a person did not have to be of any particular national, linguistic, religious, or ethnic background. All he had to do was to commit himself to the political ideology centered on the abstract ideals of liberty, equality, and republicanism. Thus the universalist ideological character of American nationality meant that it was open to anyone who willed to become an American.

About eight out of ten white Americans were actually of British derivation in 1790, and there was a latent predisposition toward an ethnically defined concept of nationality. Indeed, universalism had its limits from the beginning, because it did not include either blacks or Indians, and in time other racial and cultural groups were regarded as falling outside the range of American nationality. Yet such exclusiveness ran contrary to the logic of the defining principles, and the official commitment to those principles has worked historically to overcome exclusions and to make the practical boundaries of American identity more congruent with its theoretical universalism.

Newness was the second significant mark of American nationality. Despite a long colonial past, the origin of the American nation could be definitively assigned to the Revolution and the establishment of a unified government in the 1780s, events that constituted a decisive break with the past. America had turned its back on Europe and proclaimed itself the new order of the ages, the model for the future. The heroes in the national pantheon were the men who had brought this new order into being, the founding fathers. Other symbols of national identity—such as Independence Day, the Declaration, and the Constitution and Bill of Rights —were all associated with the classic time when the new nation had been formed.

The third mark of American nationality, future orientation, is closely related to the second, for the great accomplishments of the revolutionary generation were but a founding, a beginning. What they had created was handed on not only as a glorious heritage but also as a task, a sacred trust. To be true to their national identity, Americans had to make good the aspiration expressed in the founding documents. The differences of opinion that arose almost immediately when the federal system was set in motion made clear how arduous this struggle would be. Americans quickly realized they were far from realizing the abstract excellence of their system. Joel Barlow put it neatly in 1809: "As a nation, we are not up to our circumstance." The full realization of national identity lay in the future.

Compared to the ideological quality, emphasis on newness, and future orientation, the ethnic element in American nationality was quite recessive in the first years of the republic. This may be seen by looking briefly at a classic statement made in 1782 about ethnicity and nationality and by considering some of the practical questions related to naturalization and political controversy in the 1790s.

The classic statement is Michel-Guillaume Jean de Crève-coeur's *Letters from an American Farmer*, first published in London in 1782 but largely written in the decade before the Revolution. A landmark in American literature, Crève-coeur's *Letters* is equally famous for its formulation of yeoman-farmer agrarianism and for the enunciation of the so-called melting-pot idea of immigrant assimilation and American nationality. In a passage that has probably been quoted more often than any other in the literature of immigration, Crèvecoeur highlighted the elements of newness and future orientation in stating the assimilationist view:

What then is the American, this new man? He is either a European or the descendant of a European, hence that strange mixture of blood, which you will find in no other country. I could point out to you a family whose grandfather was an Englishman, whose wife was Dutch, whose son married a French woman, and whose present four sons have four wives of different nations. *He* is an American, who, leaving behind him all his ancient prejudices and manners, receives new ones from the new mode of life he has embraced, the new government he obeys, and the new rank he holds. He becomes an American by being received into the broad lap of our great *Alma Mater*. Here individuals are melted into a new race of men, whose labours and posterity will one day cause great changes in the world.

Here and elsewhere Crèvecoeur stressed the ethnic and religious diversity of the American population, but he was actually far less interested in what the American people had been than in what they were becoming and would be in the future. Ethnic diversity, though notable, was not so much an essential feature of the national identity as a condition that America transformed in the process of creating a new nationality. Americans would still be a new people, although probably not the same kind of new people, even if all of them had been purely English in background.

Although he stressed the elements of newness and future orientation, Crèvecoeur was less explicit about the ideological dimension, perhaps because the work was written before independence was an accomplished fact and because Crèvecoeur tended toward loyalism in his political sympathies. Yet his discussion implicitly endorsed the American ideology by its heavy emphasis on the importance of social equality and mobility in "regenerating" the poor of Europe and making them into freemen. By following his own self-interest, Crèvecoeur affirmed, a man could be transformed into an American, improve his material situation, and live a life of simplicity and virtue. The elements of the American dream were all there, not expounded as theory but asserted as practical facts and illustrated in the story of Andrew the Hebridean, whose rise from oppression to freedom, "from obscurity . . . to some degree of consequence," concluded Crèvecoeur's treatment of the question, "What is an American?"

Turning to the place of immigration and naturalization in the politics of the 1790s, we find again that the ideological dimension was more prominent than the ethnic. There is no question that the perception of linguistic and cultural differences, as well as traditional suspicions and animosities, played a role in the controversies over naturalization and the political activities of aliens and immigrants, but these considerations were definitely secondary. Moreover, the policy on naturalization that ultimately emerged from these controversies and remained in force until the early 20th century bespoke great confidence in the power of American principles, institutions, and environment to transform foreigners into acceptable Americans within a brief period and without systematic indoctrination.

The question of how foreigners could be admitted to citizenship and thus officially become Americans was taken up in the first Congress that met under the federal Constitution. There were differences of view when it was debated, with New Englanders showing a greater spirit of exclusiveness than men from the middle colonies, but the naturalization law of 1790 was extremely liberal. Even so, some republicans considered the two-year waiting period before an immigrant could become a citizen a requirement lacking in "general philanthropy."

When naturalization was brought up again in the closing days of 1794, the political climate was more highly charged. Divisions over domestic issues, such as Alexander Hamilton's fiscal program, overlapped with sharp disagreements on foreign policy, while the ideological passions aroused by the French Revolution and the outbreak of war in Europe linked these internal quarrels to the clash of irreconcilable principles across the seas. The two incipient political parties —the Federalists, centered in New England, and the Republicans, led by Thomas Jefferson and James Madison—differed in their sympathies toward the French Revolution and in their approach to domestic and foreign policy issues, but each had reason to be uneasy about some of the immigrants coming into the country as a result of the revolutionary upheavals. The Federalists were most concerned about the prominence of radical refugees from the British Isles in the ranks of their Republican opponents. They therefore pushed for an extension of the waiting period for naturalization and wanted two credible witnesses to swear to the good character of an applicant for citizenship. The Republicans, although opposed to the measure, had their own suspicions of royalist émigrés from the Revolution and succeeded in attaching to the naturalization law of 1795 a provision requiring an applicant to give up any hereditary title before he could become a U.S. citizen.

Although the law of 1795 extended the waiting period to five years, it did not provide the safeguards the Federalists considered necessary in the political crisis that arose over the XYZ Affair and the quasi-war with France. Fear of immigrant radicals and alien activists of a Jacobin hue prompted the passage of the notorious Alien and Sedition Acts of 1798, which provided for the deportation of potentially dangerous aliens and for the imprisonment of anyone making false or malicious statements about the incumbent administration or Congress. These acts also included the naturalization law of 1798, which marked a sharp departure from the previously established policy by requiring 14 years of residence before an immigrant could be admitted to citizenship, thus effectively disfranchising adult immigrants for a very extended period.

The Alien and Sedition Acts were so obviously a political weapon against the Republicans and were enforced in so partisan a manner that they backfired against the Federalists; the widespread reaction damaged the party badly in the 1800 election and contributed to Jefferson's victory. With the Republicans in office, the naturalization requirements were restored by an act of 1802 to those prevailing before the alien and sedition crisis. No major changes in the procedure were made until 1906, when the whole process of naturalization was overhauled. Thus during a century of massive immigration, any free white immigrant could become a U.S. citizen simply by swearing that he had lived in the United States for five years, that he renounced all hereditary titles and political allegiance to any other state, and that he would support the U.S. Constitution.

As these simple requirements make clear, acquisition in law of an American identity was a matter of adherence to the political values embodied in the Constitution and repudiation of all other political loyalties. The ease with which these standards could be met and the absence of adequate machinery to check the applicant's statements testified to confidence that a free, white person could become an American no matter what his national background or language. Both the character of the requirements for naturalization and the fact that the immigration controversies in the 1790s revolved around political issues support the contention that—except in the area of race—American national identity was conceived in the earliest days in abstract ideological terms much more than in ethnic terms.

A negative factor helping to make possible this concentration on the ideological aspect was the low immigration of the period. The best estimate is that only about 250,000 immigrants came to the United States in the quarter-century after the inauguration of the federal government. Without steady reinforcement from abroad, the non-English-speaking population became palpably Americanized in language. The next century, however, showed that greater immigration would bring more distinctively ethnic elements to the forefront.

Religion in American Identity, 1815–1860

The years between the end of the War of 1812 and the outbreak of the Civil War were marked by extremely rapid growth, both in territory and in population, and by dizzying social and economic change. Intensified nationalism accompanied westward expansion, giving rise in the 1840s to the bombastic doctrine of Manifest Destiny, yet expansion also heightened sectional tension by intensifying the opposition of North and South over the question of slavery in the territories. The sectional issue was by far the more important in regard to national identity; ultimately it exploded in violence, testing the Union by a four-year war. Yet the massive immigration that began in the 1830s also had clear implications for American identity, especially because so many of the newcomers were Catholics. Anti-Catholic and anti-immigrant feeling coalesced in the 1840s and 1850s in bitter outbursts of nativism. In comparison to the earlier period, ethnically rooted cultural (or, in this case, religious) differences became more prominent in the effort to define American identity. Yet the ideological emphasis continued strong and was closely connected with the religious issue. At the same time, the question of how religious and civic identities should interact became matters of debate within the Catholic community.

The sheer increase of immigration and the sudden growth of the Catholic population were basic to these developments. After being largely cut off for a generation, immigration picked up gradually after the restoration of peace in 1815. Although observers in the 1820s were impressed by the size of immigration, the flood did not set in till after 1830. Between that date and 1845 more than a million immigrants poured into the country, and in the next ten years (1846–1855) the figure almost tripled as a result of the mass exodus set off by crop failures, famine, and other economic and political disturbances in Ireland and on the continent. By 1860 the 25 principal cities had a higher percentage of the foreign-born than they have had at any time since.

Because one-third to one-half of the immigrants were Catholics, the tremendous influx made Catholics the largest religious denomination in the country. In 1790 there were perhaps 35,000 in a total white population of 3.2 million. By 1830 their numbers had increased to something more than 300,000; in the next 30 years the Catholic population shot up three-and-a-half times faster than the total population, reaching a figure of 1.6 million in 1850 and 3.1 million in 1860. Paralleling this growth was a tremendous elaboration of Catholic institutions. By 1852, when the first Plenary Council of Baltimore brought together all the Catholic bishops in the country, there were over 30 of them (only 8 of whom were American-born), presiding over ecclesiastical jurisdictions from New England to California. The Catholic population was served by more than 1,400 priests; religious communities were multiplying rapidly, as were colleges, seminaries, parochial schools, newspapers, and Catholic societies.

Growth of this magnitude could hardly be expected to occur without creating friction in a country that had been so strongly Protestant and bitterly hostile to Catholics in the

17th and 18th centuries. Despite an improvement in feeling as a result of the alliance with Catholic France in the Revolution, the situation worsened after 1830 because the period of rapid Catholic growth coincided with a terrific burst of Protestant evangelicalism. Many revivalists saw an intimate connection between Protestantism and the national destiny, which was routinely portrayed in millennial colors. To the aroused evangelicals the existence of Catholicism was utterly incompatible with the millennial promise, so the obviously increasing strength of the Catholic church in the United States appeared to be the work of the Evil One and had to be combated vigorously. Seen in this light, the campaign against Catholicism was as much a reform drive as was the temperance crusade; both were intended to eliminate evils that militated against the coming 1,000-year reign of Christ's love.

The first episodes of anti-Catholicism in the 1830s were closely connected to the evangelical revival. A series of sermons delivered by the evangelical leader, Lyman Beecher, was widely regarded as having sparked the riotous attack that led to the burning of the Ursuline convent in Charlestown, Mass., in 1834. Anti-Catholicism springing from this source could draw on the accumulated fears and hatreds of centuries of religious strife, and it often sank to the lowest levels of vilification, as exemplified in the salacious slanders of Catholic priests and nuns in works such as Maria Monk's *Awful Disclosures of the Hotel Dieu Nunnery of Montreal* (1836).

Anti-Catholic nativism expanded from these beginnings to a climax in 1844 when the "Native American" phase of the movement erupted in Philadelphia in two episodes of rioting, each lasting several days, which cost more than a dozen lives and resulted in the burning of two Catholic churches. A temporary lull followed these frightening outbursts, but after 1850 the anti-Catholic form of nativism reached its historic high point in what was called Know-Nothingism. The Know-Nothings, a political party officially known as the

American party, developed as an offshoot of a secret patriotic society, the Order of the Star-Spangled Banner. Dedicated to extending the naturalization requirement to 21 years and excluding Catholics and the foreign-born from holding office, the Know-Nothings reached the peak of their influence in 1855 when they controlled 6 states (Massachusetts, Connecticut, Rhode Island, New Hampshire, Maryland, and Kentucky) and sent some 75 representatives to Congress. The movement, accompanied by sporadic episodes of violence, declined quickly after 1856 as sectional tension over slavery overshadowed all other issues.

Anti-Catholicism was basic to these developments, but ante-bellum nativism also reflected a fundamental concern with national identity. The question that bothered the Native Americans and Know-Nothings might be expressed in colloquial terms as, "Whose country is this, anyhow?" They were disturbed and angry because the vast influx of Catholic foreigners not only challenged the hegemony of Protestantism, but seemed to threaten republican principles, the political process, the educational system, and prevailing cultural and behavioral norms.

Three widely circulated works of the mid-1830s played a key role in linking anti-Catholicism with fear of immigration and in highlighting the ideological threat represented by the growing strength of the Catholic church. In his *Foreign Conspiracy against the Liberties of the United States* (1834) and its sequel, *Imminent Dangers to the Free Institutions of the United States through Foreign Immigration* (1835), Samuel F.B. Morse argued that Catholic immigration was being deliberately stimulated and guided to the United States by the reactionary powers of Europe, especially Austria, as part of a calculated design to weaken republicanism and thereby frustrate "the onward march of the world to liberty." Morse singled out the Catholic mission-aid societies in Europe as evidence of such a plot, laying particular stress on the Leopoldine Society, founded in Vienna in 1829 and named after the daughter of the Austrian emperor. Lyman Beecher's *A Plea for the*

West (1835) developed the same general line of argument, except that he stressed the Ohio Valley, rapidly filling with immigrants, as the crucial area of competition between Protestant republicanism and Catholic-immigrant despotism.

Although the contention that Catholicism was despotic was not new, it became more timely and urgent, not only because of the swelling numbers of American Catholics, but also because of the spectacular resurgence of European Catholicism that accompanied the Romantic movement and the restoration of legitimist regimes after the downfall of Napoleon. In the polarization between liberalism and republicanism, on the one hand, and conservatism and royalism, on the other, the Catholic church in Europe was definitely aligned with the latter. The prospects for rapprochement were worsened by the revolutions of 1848, which transformed Pope Pius IX from a moderate progressive into a rigorous reactionary. Hence the uprisings of 1848, which Americans generally approved of, tended to confirm their view that Catholics were dangerously antirepublican. The clash was dramatized by the reception accorded Louis Kossuth when the Hungarian revolutionary leader visited the United States in 1851: he was lionized by American liberals, but denounced by Catholic spokesmen as a "Red Republican" symbol of atheism and anarchy. The passions associated with 1848 also inflamed the visit in 1853–1854 of the papal nuncio, Gaetano Bedini, who was defamed, hung in effigy, and physically endangered by mobs in several American cities for his alleged role in putting down the revolution in Bologna.

One aim of Bedini's visit had been to settle the worst of the old disputes over "trusteeism" in Catholic congregations, the conflicts between bishops and lay trustees over control of church property. Rebellious trustees usually claimed to be trying to introduce a more republican system of internal administration to the Catholic church, and they often welcomed the aid of nativists. By involving himself in this issue Bedini lent plausibility to the charge that Catholics were dominated by foreign princes. Thus, though trust-eeism was an internal issue of church discipline, it touched on republican values in a manner that fed nativist suspicions.

In politics the conduct of Catholics and immigrants also gave serious offense; although Germans came in for their share of suspicion, the Irish were regarded as the chief offenders. They were the most numerous and conspicuous of the Catholic immigrants; they were concentrated in the great eastern cities; they spoke English and were already politicized to some extent before emigrating; they were extremely active in party politics, usually as Democrats; and they were associated with some of the worst political abuses of the day. Because of their lack of habituation in republican virtues, it was said, the immigrants were easily manipulated; they voted in blocs at the behest of their priests or political bosses and were involved in all manner of fraudulent practices. Immigrants were sworn in as citizens before meeting the residence requirement; they were "colonized," sent to vote in districts where reinforcements were needed although they did not live there; and they were believed to be responsible for much of the physical intimidation and violence at polling places. For all these reasons, the nativists concluded that U.S. politics could never be restored to true republican purity until the immigrants were eliminated by extension of the waiting period for naturalization to 21 years and restriction of office holding to the native-born.

Irish immigrants also aroused misgivings because of their noisy agitation on behalf of homeland causes like Daniel O'Connell's Repeal Movement or, a few years later, Fenianism. But this type of political activism, although it suggested to nativists an undue attachment to the homeland, was not nearly so repugnant as the organized political efforts by Catholics to get public funds for their schools. Education was perhaps the most highly charged issue of all, bringing together in a single focus all the passions associated with religious belief, moral theory, ideological conviction, political sensitivity, parental affection, and concern for future generations.

The development of the common school paralleled the massive ante-bellum immigration and the striking growth of the Catholic church. The parallelism was not wholly fortuitous, for the common school was intended, among other things, to meet and overcome the potentially disintegrative influences flowing from immigration and Catholic growth. The developing public schools, in other words, were supposed to serve an Americanizing function, and the version of Americanism they symbolized integrated a nondenominational Protestant outlook in religion and morality with a republican viewpoint in political principle and practice. Evangelical leaders like Calvin Stowe (the son-in-law of Lyman Beecher) played a crucial role in promoting the common schools, and a Protestant consensus in education was widely regarded as essential to the preservation of genuine Americanism. Seen against this background, the establishment of separate Catholic schools was bound to arouse hostility, and Catholic efforts to gain public funds seemed a form of *lèse majesté*.

Catholic schools were objectionable in themselves, because they were looked upon as perpetuating religious error and inculcating an antirepublican mentality, but the first major battle in a tradition of controversy that has continued to the present day was set off in 1840 when Bishop John Hughes of New York tried to win public funds for Catholic schools. Although it was Governor William Seward who first broached the matter of public support for Catholic schools, Hughes's campaign of lobbying, political pressure, and mobilization of Catholic voters outraged Protestants and confirmed nativists in the conviction that Catholicism was intolerable politically as well as educationally. Additional bitter controversy arose over Catholic objections to the reading of the King James version of the Bible in the common schools, an issue deeply involved in the anti-Catholic riots in Philadelphia in 1844. And a concerted effort by Catholics in several states for a share of the school fund was part of the immediate background to the emergence of Know-Nothingism in the early 1850s.

Besides being objectionable on religious and political grounds, parochial schools reflected a Catholic clannishness and separatism that aroused resentment among the Protestant majority. Similarly the strangeness of the immigrants' costume, language, accent, and manners struck the natives unfavorably. The poverty of many immigrants, especially those fleeing from Ireland in the famine years, the squalid, overcrowded quarters in which many of them had to live, and the debauchery and drunkenness that flourished in such surroundings also contributed to the impression that immigration was degrading American character and morals. The weakness of the Irish for drink, associated as it was with riotously boisterous "Paddy funerals" and all manner of brawls, was particularly damning because the temperance movement had early taken on symbolic importance as a crusade to preserve the moral character of American society.

The flood of immigration thus raised questions about the national identity from the perspectives of religion, ideology, politics, education, and general culture. It was the presence of vast numbers of Catholic immigrants, more than anything else, that brought religious and ethnic considerations into the discussion of what it meant to be an American. The full proscriptive program of the Know-Nothings, a coalition hung precariously around anti-Catholicism and antiforeignism, was nowhere enacted, but the fear of and hostility toward Catholicism that it mobilized remained active in American politics for the next century.

Besides creating external opposition, the Know-Nothings also precipitated an internal debate among Catholics over how the church should adjust to the novel environment of the United States. The first explicit intra-Catholic controversy over Americanization occurred in the middle 1850s, although Catholic interest in this question dated back to the earliest days of the new republic. John Carroll, the first Catholic bishop, came from an old Maryland family and was keenly sensitive to the need to bring the church into line with American institutions. Later Catholic leaders shared Carroll's approval of the American system of separation of church and state and of governmental noninterference in religious affairs. Catholics took pride in the role played by their coreligionists in the exploration and settlement of the country, especially in the pioneering example of religious toleration furnished by the Catholic colony of Maryland. Formal commemoration of the landing of the Maryland colonists began in the 1840s in order to highlight the Catholic contribution to American religious freedom.

Official statements by churchmen inculcated civic loyalty and devotion to the Constitution. On occasion, Catholic spokesmen also took note of the dangers of isolating themselves from the rest of the community, especially in nationalistic, rather than religious, societies. The Boston *Pilot*, an Irish Catholic paper, spoke out in 1854 against the kind of groups that gave the impression that the Irish were "a community and army *encamped* merely upon a foreign ground." Bishop Hughes in New York publicly opposed Irish colonization projects for similar reasons. Nor did church leaders fail to criticize immigrant customs that attracted unfavorable notice from natives, for example, boisterous wakes and funerals, of which the *Pilot* said in 1849: "The old habits of Ireland will not answer here."

But despite the earlier history of concern over these issues, the relationship of Americanism and Catholicism assumed a new level of self-consciousness and importance in the 1850s. The first reason was obviously nativism, which Catholics could not ignore even if they wanted to. Second, the overwhelming immigration of the 1840s and 1850s brought in a multitude of Catholics who tended to identify their religion with their former nationality. This was as true of the Germans as of the Irish, but because the latter were more numerous and conspicuous, the chief practical result was a tendency to equate Catholicism with being Irish and Protestantism with being American.

The unwisdom of any such association was clear to most church leaders on the theoretical level, but it was personally offensive to Orestes A. Brownson, the most prominent of a group of notable American converts to Catholicism. A Vermont Yankee by birth, Brownson was affronted by immigrant Catholic sneers at "Natyvism" and by what he perceived as an active dislike of the American people and character on the part of many Catholic leaders. He also felt a strong aversion for the Irish on social and cultural grounds, referring to them in his private correspondence in very unflattering terms. What troubled him most, however, was the implicit assumption that Irish and Catholic were interchangeable terms. Brownson was very sympathetic to the view of his friend and fellow-convert, Isaac Hecker, that Americans were a deeply religious people who would respond eagerly to Catholicism if it were presented to them in a congenial manner.

These factors prompted the appearance of two articles in the July 1854 issue of *Brownson's Quarterly Review*, "Schools and Education" and "Native Americanism," which opened the first Catholic debate on Americanization. Brownson followed up in October with "The Know Nothings," in which he defended himself against the criticism called forth by the previous articles. Related pieces appeared from time to time over the next several years, one of which contained the first use of the word "Americanization," according to *A Dictionary of American English on Historical Principles*.

Brownson's position in the controversy was strongly assimilationist. Although he admitted that the two had become intermixed, Brownson insisted that nativism was not the same as anti-Catholicism. He rejected the latter, of course, but said that nativism should be understood as a legitimate expression of nationality on the part of Americans who loved their homeland. A people with as much national pride as the Irish, he remarked, ought to be able to understand the same feeling in Americans. They would also have to accept the fact that the American nationality had already been formed in a basically Anglo-Saxon mold, and that the

immigrants must conform to it because no deliberate perpetuation of foreign nationalities on American soil would be
tolerated. Because this kind of Americanism was the appropriate nationality for the country and because it would pre-
vail, it would clearly be suicidal for the Catholic religion to
allow itself to be identified with any foreign nationality.
Hence it was imperative to distinguish between nationality
and Catholicity, so that immigrants would not abandon
their faith in the process of Americanizing, and Americans
would understand that to become a Catholic one did not
have to give up his nationality.

In politics the real immigrant threat, in Brownson's view,
came not from Catholics but from the radical extremists who
had fled from the unsuccessful European uprisings of 1848.
Nevertheless he agreed that naturalization was a "boon"
rather than a natural right and that the franchise should be
reserved to the American-born. He also warned Irish nationalists against mobilizing in the United States for homeland
causes. In education Brownson regretted that anti-Catholicism made it necessary to maintain a system of separate
schools and argued that Catholics could gain much from the
public schools because of their Americanizing tendency and
because the faith of Catholic children would be strengthened
by early contact with Protestants, provided their parents and
pastors took pains to instruct them outside the school. Later
Brownson also criticized Catholic colleges and seminaries
for reflecting an Old-World mentality and failing to prepare
their students for the kind of problems they would face in
the United States.

Many Irish and Catholic spokesmen were outraged by
Brownson's blast, and others regarded it as ill-timed. The
reaction led him to clarify his position and to emphasize the
essential point that Catholicism was not to be identified
with *any* nationality; he believed that an emphatic statement
was needed to bring this home both to immigrant Catholics
and to Protestant Americans. This rhetorical need, along
with Brownson's personal antipathy for the Irish, accounted

for the harshness of his 1854 statement. In other contexts he emphasized different aspects of the subject. But Brownson did not retreat from his contention that Catholicism in the United States must cut itself free from identification with the Old World and be brought into line with American norms and values wherever that could be done without threat to the faith. If the church were to be true to its universal mission, it had to be at home in all cultures. Brownson's perception that this required a kind of Americanization set off a brief flurry in the 1850s, anticipating the controversies that rocked the American Catholic community 30 years later over the German nationality question, education, and theological Americanism. Thus the relationship of religion to nationality became an explosive issue among American Catholics just as it was between Catholics and the larger community.

Ethnicity in American Identity (1860–1924)

Although the religious element in ethnicity emerged as an issue in the first half of the 19th century, other cultural, or what used to be called "racial," elements did not become central to the discussion of American nationality until the latter decades of the century. The Civil War reawakened nationalism and solidified the identification between the Union and liberty, but immigration and ethnic differentiation played very little part in this. The participation of immigrants in the Union armies reduced suspicion of the foreign-born, and although anti-Catholicism flared up more than once after the war, it was never again the primary focus for a general nativist movement. Other issues, such as Reconstruction policy and economic expansion, took center stage after Appomattox, and immigrants were welcomed to fill the labor needs of a rapidly industrializing nation. The volume of immigration mounted in the later decades of the century and rose to unprecedented heights after 1900, but by this time, immigration had again become controversial. It was associated with a variety of social problems and regarded as undesirable in itself. Unlike the Civil War, World War I fueled ethnic animosities, with the result that soon after peace returned, a series of restrictionist laws cut back immigration sharply. The reversal of the nation's historic policy of free immigration was the most important result of the debate carried on from the 1890s to the 1920s. There was also a theoretical legacy, because several of the terms in which subsequent discussion of ethnicity and national identity has been carried on emerged in this era.

The Melting Pot

This term, which remains the most popular symbol for ethnic interaction and the society in which it takes place, was launched by Israel Zangwill's play *The Melting-Pot*, which had a long run in New York in 1909. Zangwill was an English Jew who adopted the expression "melting pot" from its conventional usage in England as a metaphor for the process of fundamental transformation. Before Zangwill's play the expression was not common in the United States; since then it has been used almost exclusively to refer to ethnicity and intergroup relations.

Zangwill's play tells of an idealistic young Jewish immigrant who believes that Old-World nationalities should be forgotten in the United States and that all elements should fuse together in the creation of a new and superior American nationality. These ideas were very old; in one sense all Zangwill did was furnish a new symbol for a set of loose, informal notions (which had long been associated with terms like "melting," "blending," "fusing," and the like) about America's great powers of assimilation, powers that had traditionally been thought of as operating automatically. At the same time the symbol of the melting pot invited an interpretation of assimilation as a purposeful process of burning off impurities and molding immigrants to a predetermined type.

The best-known early statement of the traditional view is that of Crèvecoeur, the key passage of which has already been quoted. Although he did not use the expression "melting pot," Crèvecoeur did speak of persons from many nations being "melted into a new race of men," and it is quite appropriate to regard his discussion as the classic formulation of what might be called the cosmopolitan-nationality version of the melting-pot theme. As John Higham has pointed out, the motto *"E pluribus unum"* summed up "the essence of America's cosmopolitan faith—a conviction that this new land would bring unity out of diversity as a matter of course." This was the majority view through the 19th century, reaffirmed against the nativists of the 1840s and 1850s by Ralph Waldo Emerson and others; when it appeared in Zangwill's play, audiences responded to what one critic called a drama "touched with the fire of democracy, and lighted radiantly with the national vision."

The critic's language was legitimate, because of the close congruence between the cosmopolitan-nationality version of the melting-pot idea and the national ideology, with its abstract universalism, its emphasis on newness, and its orientation toward the future. The melting pot paralleled these points in its undiscriminating acceptance of newcomers who were willing to identify themselves with American principles, commit themselves to a new life in the new land, and labor for a better future for their children and grandchildren. It was minimalist in what it asked the immigrant to do in order to become an American and optimistic in the expectation that his experience in the new homeland would solidify his commitment to the principles of American democracy. This version of the melting pot also assumed that the conditions of American life, particularly egalitarianism and the opportunity for material improvement, would automatically transform foreigners into Americans—with some help from the common schools. Another thread in this complex of ideas was the belief that the emerging American nationality would be enriched by the diversity of the ethnic elements that composed it. By the 1850s scientific arguments of a

Spencerian or Darwinian sort were occasionally offered in support of the theory that mixed peoples were superior to those of a single strain.

Yet with all its liberality and tolerance, the cosmopolitan version of the melting pot was still a theory of assimilation. The idea that the immigrants must change was basic; they were to become new people. The American identity might not be fully formed, but it was far from indeterminate. Some of its features were established by the basic political ideology; others were more vague, deriving in a tacit manner from the majority culture and the evolving experience of the national community. This was the nationality into which the immigrants and their children were expected to merge. In doing so they would enrich it, refine it, or modify it in detail, but no one anticipated fundamental revision. And of course there were racial limitations: blacks and Indians were excluded from the outset, and Asiatics after 1882, when a new law banned the immigration of Chinese laborers.

From Crèvecoeur's time until late in the 19th century, most Americans supported this version of melting-pot thinking, and even the growing Anglo-Saxonism of the post-Civil War years at first reinforced it. The Anglo-Saxons were touted as a people distinguished by their capacity to assimilate others, absorbing their desirable qualities without being basically changed themselves. But confidence in America's absorptive capacities was essential to the continued viability of this laissez-faire melting-pot thinking. From the 1880s on, increasing numbers of Americans came to doubt that the mysterious alembic of American society was actually functioning as it was supposed to—too many immigrants were coming into the country; they were coming too fast; they were too different from the American national type to be assimilated painlessly or even, many felt, to be assimilated at all.

When Zangwill's play appeared, a minority of Americans still retained their confidence in the nation's absorptive powers, but they were soon swamped by those who believed that the situation required, at the very least, a more active policy of purposeful Americanization. The title of the play supplied a perfect symbol, not only for the traditional cosmopolitan-nationalists, but also for those who wanted to intervene more actively in the processes of assimilation. Did not a melting pot require watching? Might it not become overheated? What was to be done about the dross and slag that were waste products of its operation? Metaphorical elaboration along these lines and the use of the melting-pot symbol by the fervid 100-percent Americanizers of the World War I epoch tended to submerge the earlier strain of tolerant cosmopolitanism; especially among liberals, the melting pot came to be associated with a repugnant, forced-assimilation approach.

In the 1920s the symbol of the melting pot was discredited, not only among liberals, but also among ultranationalists, who decided that even its superheated version had not worked. Although still popular in journalistic usage, the term did not figure prominently in serious discussions of intergroup relations for a number of years. It was to some degree revived and rehabilitated by Will Herberg's *Protestant-Catholic-Jew* (1955), which popularized the notion that the "three great faiths of democracy" constituted a "triple melting pot." But the symbol was subjected to a barrage of unfavorable commentary in the ethnic revival of the 1960s and 1970s. Nathan Glazer and Daniel Moynihan's *Beyond the Melting Pot* (1963), an early landmark, set the tone for much later usage in announcing that "The point about the melting pot is that it did not happen." Later spokesmen for the new ethnicity treated the melting pot as a symbol of everything hateful in the nation's record on immigration and intergroup relations.

However, these writers seem unable to talk about the subject without using the expression melting pot. They have thus given it a more central place in discussions of ethnicity and nationality than it has had at any time since World War I. Their unrelievedly negative and hostile interpretation of the symbol has also reproduced the set of relationships that developed in that era when the melting pot was identified with forced Americanization and contrasted with cultural pluralism.

Americanization

This term, in its generic sense roughly equivalent to assimilation, became attached to a specific movement in the first two decades of the 20th century; its meaning since then has been colored to some extent by identification with the movement. The words "Americanize," "Americanizing," and "Americanization," were all in common usage during the ante-bellum nativist controversies, clearly referring to the immigrants' becoming assimilated into American life. However, there was disagreement as to precisely what the process required. The Irish, who were being urged by Brownson to Americanize, inquired of him what pattern of Americanism they were to conform to—that of New England, Virginia, or Kentucky. They also insisted that some forms of Americanization, such as heedless materialism and mammon-worship, were unwholesome.

Just what it means to become or to be an American is the central question concerning the national identity. Some have interpreted true Americanism as requiring close conformity to the cultural majority in language, religion, and manners, while others have adopted a more relaxed position about the range of variation that could be accommodated within the national identity. In the late 19th century, along with the shift in thinking about the melting pot, the balance swung toward the former view, as more Americans began to feel the nation required a higher level of cohesion and solidarity.

In part the shift resulted from the increasingly visible presence of the new immigrants crowding into the cities from eastern and southern Europe. These Italians, Slavs, and Jews not only seemed more alien than earlier immigrants in their language and culture, they were also linked in the public mind with strikes, social unrest, and urban problems such as crime and slum housing. Also involved was the development of a more ethnically restrictive, Anglo-Saxon version of American nationality. As Anglo-Saxon racialism waxed, it became easier to persuade Americans that other groups needed more systematic assistance in emulating the virtues of the older stock.

These two considerations operated powerfully in the minds of those who interpreted Americanism in narrow terms and who believed that Americanization was needed to protect the national character from the dangers posed by the immense immigration of the times. Other Americanizers, however, were animated by a more positive desire to assist the immigrants in adjusting to the strange and often harsh conditions of life they encountered in the United States. This group represented a continuation of the older tradition of cosmopolitan nationalism. The Americanization movement included both of these orientations, but as it developed from about 1900 to the early 1920s the former emphasis became more dominant, eventually giving the whole movement a repressive and nativistic tone.

The Americanization movement passed through three phases: the first extended from around the turn of the century to 1914; the second covered the years of World War I; the third, the immediate postwar years. In the first phase, the nervously nationalistic strain was represented by such patriotic groups as the Daughters of the American Revolution (DAR) and by the Boston-based North American Civic League for Immigrants, founded in 1908. On the other hand, settlement-house workers, advocates of the social gospel, and others committed to progressivism stressed the need for protective legislation for immigrants and took a positive view of the cultural contributions they could make to American life. Both groups sought a more harmoniously integrated society.

Differences in approach and shifts in emphasis were par-

ticularly evident in the area of education. The importance of
the public school in bringing together the children of diverse
ethnic strains and teaching them the responsibilities of U.S.
citizenship had been recognized from the earliest days.
What was new in the Progressive period was heightened
self-consciousness and a greater sense of urgency about
these matters. But agreement that the schools played a vital
role did not imply agreement about how they should go
about it or the spirit in which it should be undertaken. To a
racialist like Elwood P. Cubberly, a well-known educational
historian, the task was "to implant in their [the immigrants']
children, so far as can be done, the Anglo-Saxon conception
of righteousness, law and order, and popular government;
and to awaken in them a reverence for our democratic institutions and for those things in our national life which we as
a people hold to be of abiding worth." At the other extreme
John Dewey prescribed cosmopolitanism as the correct "na-
tionalizing" policy for the public schools. It was the responsibility of the schools, he told the National Education Association in 1916, to "teach each [ethnic] factor to respect every
other, and . . . to enlighten all as to the great contributions
of every strain in our composite make-up."

Instruction in hygiene, domestic science, and industrial
arts was also linked to Americanization at the level of practical school programs, but the principal new departure was in
adult education for immigrants. Special classes were offered
both by settlement houses and by patriotic groups; the
YMCA entered the field in 1907 with evening courses in English and civics, the two subjects most heavily stressed.

The ethnic reverberation set off in the United States by the
outbreak of the European war in 1914 marked the opening of
a far more intense phase of the Americanization movement.
The return to Europe of thousands of immigrants who were
reservists in the armies of the belligerents and the eruption
of ethnic nationalism on the part of immigrant groups with
close ties to the warring powers came as a shock to many
Americans, who had not realized just how "foreign" the

sentiments and attachments of the foreign-born population actually were. Sensational exposés of German propaganda and sabotage efforts in the United States, coming on the heels of the *Lusitania* crisis, reinforced anti-German sentiment and gave rise to a formidable campaign against "hyphenation." The hyphen in such compounds as German-American was regarded as symbolizing divided loyalties, and "100 percent Americanism" became the goal of Americanization programs.

The wartime Americanization campaign reached its climax during the years of U.S. involvement in the fighting, but several significant changes were evident by 1915. First, the number of agencies and organizations supporting the movement expanded greatly, as did the frequency and visibility of its activities and the level of mass support they received. By 1915 the U.S. Bureau of Education and the U.S. Bureau of Naturalization were actively involved; after 1917 the Committee on Public Information also took part. State and local governmental bodies pitched in, joined by innumerable private groups, chambers of commerce, advocates of "preparedness," and special organizations, the most important of which was the National Americanization Committee (NAC).

The NAC, which evolved out of earlier organizations dedicated to a cosmopolitan-nationalist, reform-oriented approach, illustrates the second significant change in this phase of the movement. Its director, Frances A. Kellor, had a background in social work and strong progressive commitments. Aptly described as "half reformer, half nationalist," by 1915 Kellor had allowed her national inclinations to take charge, although they were still integrated with a Rooseveltian, progressive belief in efficiency, scientific planning, and rational control. Under her leadership the NAC moved clearly in the direction of forced assimilation, and Kellor's 1916 book, *Straight America*, argued that military preparedness, industrial mobilization, universal service, and Americanization were all essential to a more vital nationalism.

Kellor and the NAC were also deeply involved in a third significant feature of wartime Americanization, the widespread participation in the movement of manufacturers who employed immigrants. Usually courses in English and citizenship were grafted on to existing programs of welfare work or industrial betterment, which had been gaining ground since the turn of the century. They were products of the emerging subprofession of personnel management, and though an expression of enlightened self-interest on the part of employers, the health and safety education programs and the general improvement of working conditions in the plant also benefited workers. The addition of Americanization classes may be thought of as bringing to a new level of self-consciousness the linkage between assimilation to American culture and the acclimation of preindustrial immigrants to factory discipline, which has been a recurrent feature of American social history.

Americanization reached its most feverish level in the third phase of the movement, which occurred in the context of postwar fear of social revolution. While antiradicalism reached panic level in the Red Scare, patriotic groups intensified their Americanization programs to inoculate the great mass of the immigrants against the revolutionary contagion being spread by the radical few. Businessmen were deeply involved in these programs, and Americanization became closely identified with welfare capitalism and antiunionism. But business leaders were generally more moderate than groups such as the National Security League and the American Legion. Strongly nativistic, they called for the deportation of alien radicals and resorted to high-pressure propaganda tactics. Many state and local authorities stepped up their efforts by restricting the use of languages other than English in the schools, by requiring public school teachers to be American citizens, and (in an Oregon law declared unconstitutional in 1925) by compelling all elementary-age children to attend public schools.

The relatively few liberals who had taken the sympathetic "immigrant gifts" approach to Americanization withdrew in disgust at the reactionary chauvinism of the movement in the postwar years. Immigrant spokesmen likewise openly expressed their resentment of cultural aggression against their language and customs in the name of Americanization, which in its last phase was thought of almost exclusively in narrow and nativistic terms. The Ku Klux Klan's appropriation of the term Americanism reinforced the same association and further discredited the whole idea.

The major legacy of the movement was to make Americanization a bad word, even in its generic sense of assimilation. Although this development was understandable, it created a problem in respect to national identity, because it made the national name disreputable. It also gave rise to a situation in which those who resisted Americanization on the practical level (as assimilation) and reviled it as an idea could claim to be the truest Americanists of all. This is roughly what happened after the introduction of the idea of cultural pluralism, which implied resistance in practice and rejection in principle of Americanization as assimilation. One reason that cultural pluralism seemed so attractive by contrast was that Americanization had been closely linked to Anglo-Saxon racialism and was therefore adversely affected by the reaction against racism that took root among intellectuals in the 1920s and spread to broader strata of the population in the next decades.

Anglo-Saxon Racialism

Anglo-Saxonism began as a form of ethnic pride; eventually it became, or was absorbed into, a much harsher form of racism understood as a scientific doctrine linking the qualitative status of different peoples (that is, whether they placed high or low on an absolute scale of civilization) to biologically determined factors that were passed on genetically from one generation to the next. As used here, the term "racialism" embraces both the earlier, prescientific Anglo-Saxonism and the rigid, naturalistic racism that reached a climax in the first quarter of the 20th century. Throughout its development, Anglo-Saxon racialism was intimately related to ideas of American nationality, but significant changes took place in the way the relationship was understood and the implications it was thought to have for immigration policy and intergroup relations.

The roots of Anglo-Saxonism go back to the political controversies of the English Civil War in the mid-17th century. The champions of Parliament portrayed their struggle with Charles I as a defense of the immemorial liberties of the English people against the tendencies toward royal absolutism implanted by the introduction of feudal law at the time of the Norman conquest. The contrast between the despotic "Norman yoke" and the "Gothic liberties" of Anglo-Saxon times were elaborated during the Commonwealth period and kept alive after the Stuart Restoration; this contrast became one of the elements of the "true Whig" or "country" ideology of 18th-century republicanism, both in England and in the American colonies.

Anglo-Saxonism was thus closely identified from the first with love of freedom, dedication to republicanism, and a commitment to law and limited government. Allied to these political qualities were such domestic and personal virtues as respect for womanhood, honesty, simplicity, and bravery. This ensemble remained the substantive core of Anglo-Saxonism, but it came to be understood in more distinctively racial terms; that is, a commitment to liberty and republicanism was no longer regarded merely as the political heritage of the Anglo-Saxons, but as their native genius, the form of social life and organization toward which they were innately disposed and for which they were peculiarly well suited.

Romanticism accounted for the new racial stress in Anglo-Saxonism; races or nations were thought of as collective enti-

ties with lives of their own, each having characteristic qualities—its *Volksgeist* or national soul. Romantic fascination
with these matters was reflected in early-19th-century historical studies, the study of languages and folklore, and eth-
nological curiosity about the races and cultures of man. The
romantic view of the Anglo-Saxons as a simple, upright,
freedom-loving race was popularized by Sharon Turner's
History of the Anglo-Saxons (1799–1805) and by Walter Scott's
portrayal of the clash between Saxons and Normans in *Ivan-
hoe* (1817). By mid-century, Anglo-Saxonism in England had
developed into a full-blooded racialist version of nationalism, which exalted the special virtues of the Saxons and contrasted them to the inadequacies of other races, particularly
the Celts of Ireland.

This kind of thinking was slower to develop in the United
States, an Anglo-Saxon country at one remove from the
homeland. Another possible handicap to its development
was that the most race-conscious group in America—southern slaveholders—identified themselves with the Norman
elite of post-Conquest England, rather than with the subju-
gated Saxons. Yet the mounting Anglo-Saxon enthusiasm in
England found echoes in the United States. An American
edition of Sharon Turner's history was published in 1841,
and a decade later a writer in *North American Review* observed that "of late years, we have come to call ourselves
Anglo-Saxons in common parlance." In 1843 George Perkins
Marsh traced the origins of New England institutions back
to the forests of Germany in his *Goths in New England,* com-
bining anti-Celticism and militant anti-Catholicism with his
Gothic passion. It was generally accepted that Protestantism
was the natural religious expression of the freedom-loving,
independent-thinking Anglo-Saxons, while Catholicism
was best suited to the more servile peoples who lived under
Latin forms of despotism. Even Brownson, the Catholic con-
vert, distinguished between "Romanic" and "Germanic"
traditions, the former identified with submission to the
ruler, while the latter provided for a freer kind of coopera-

tion in self-government. And as we have seen, Brownson believed that the American nationality was already set in a fundamentally Anglo-Saxon mold.

Ante-bellum Anglo-Saxonism was more closely linked with the expansionist version of American nationalism than with its nativist version. Fundamentally it was an expression of ethnic pride by the American cultural majority, those of English background who gloried in the heroic virtues and splendid achievements of their ancestors and who associated their own national accomplishments with this virile heritage. Anglo-Saxonism was interwoven with the ideological and religious aspects of the national identity. Although racial, it had more to do with a romantically understood racial "character" than with the biological transmission of fixed physical attributes. It was inclusive rather than exclusive, as the *North American Review* asserted in 1851. "We are the most mixed race that ever existed; and yet the admixture has never been such as to weaken or impoverish the original Saxon stock; on the contrary, it has infused into it new life and energy."

After the Civil War, those who were most conscious of springing from "old American stock" continued to promulgate Anglo-Saxonism as their version of ethnic nationalism. The connection between Anglo-Saxonism and the nation's free institutions was reinforced by the historical works of Edward A. Freeman, whose enthusiastic Teutonism was almost as popular in the United States as in his native England; by John Fiske, who interpreted the federal system as America's distinctive addition to the Saxon tradition of self-government; and by Herbert Baxter Adams, who made the "germ theory" of Teutonic origins the orthodox paradigm for historical investigations at Johns Hopkins University. Josiah Strong's widely read *Our Country* (1886) appealed to the Anglo-Saxon heritage as part of his effort to arouse Americans to meet their religious and patriotic responsibilities in a rapidly changing world. The association of Anglo-Saxonism with America's mission to extend the blessings of free institutions to other peoples reached a climax in turn-of-the-century imperialism.

There was in all this a clear continuity with ante-bellum Anglo-Saxonism and confidence that the incomparably vigorous Saxon race would go on extending its beneficent influence. But in the 1880s and 1890s another and more ominous strain of thought developed, which called attention to the threats to Anglo-Saxon predominance and the national identity rooted in that racial heritage. This modulation toward a defensive and hostile version of racialism, useful not merely to enhance the pride of its adherents but even more to measure the inferiority and undesirability of others, was one of two major shifts that took place in Anglo-Saxon race-thinking between the Gilded Age and World War I. In a second, closely related development, Anglo-Saxonism was linked to scientific racism, which was understood as a matter of biological and physical-anthropological determinism.

New England was the earliest center of the defensive form of racial Anglo-Saxonism, and its patrician class was at the forefront of the transition. Anxieties stemming from the economic and cultural decline of the region and the slippage in status of the Brahmin elite contributed to a growing hostility toward immigrants, whose increasing numbers, growing political influence, and discordant foreign ways made the race-proud Anglo-Saxon aristocrats feel like aliens in their own homeland. In the 1890s racialist opposition focused on the new immigrants from eastern and southern Europe. The Immigration Restriction League, founded in Boston in 1894, dedicated itself to reducing the stream of new immigrants by pushing for the enactment of a literacy test.

Although some promoters of the literacy test frankly avowed their intention to protect the Anglo-Saxon basis of American nationality from dilution by lesser breeds, it is significant that the restrictive mechanism itself—the literacy test—was not explicitly racial. Openly racial restrictive criteria were not incorporated into legislation until the 1920s; the rapid dissemination of scientific racism, coupled with the blending of race-thinking and panicky xenophobia in the early 1920s, made possible the enactment of the national-origins quota system in 1924. Racial ideas had taken on scientific coloring earlier through association with notions of evolutionary progress, especially with the Spencerian version of social Darwinism, understood as a competitive struggle among different social groups for survival and dominance. After 1900, however, scientific racism became notably more precise and stringent through the popularization of Mendelian genetics in biology and the physiographic measurement and classification of races carried out by anthropologists.

William Z. Ripley's *Races of Europe* (1899) synthesized the anthropological studies and supplied a threefold classification of European peoples into the Teutonic, Alpine, and Mediterranean races. Ripley himself was only a mild Teutonist and stressed environmental, rather than hereditary, factors in accounting for differences between races. But his typology accorded nicely with the traditional distinctions used by those who preached a stark Teutonic supremacy, and it fitted the needs of restrictionists who wished to protect Anglo-Saxon culture from the contamination of inferior Alpine and Mediterranean stocks. It was commonly assumed at the time that cultural traits were inherited along with physical attributes, and the restrictionists drew impressive support from the new science of eugenics for their view that the indiscriminate mixing of races was more likely to result in cultural debasement than cultural improvement.

Racialist doctrine was given its most systematic and influential statement in Madison Grant's *The Passing of the Great Race*, published in 1916. For Grant, "race pure and simple, the physical and psychical structures of man" lay at the basis of every manifestation of human creativity, and the Nordic was "the master race" that had led humanity upward since the dawn of civilization. He flatly denied the traditional American premise of equality, characterized the idea of the melting pot as "folly," and warned Americans that "this generation must completely repudiate the proud boast of our fathers that they acknowledged no distinction in 'race, creed, or color.'" Grant made no effort to conceal his hatred and contempt for the "human flotsam" of the new immigration. He regarded as "pathetic and fatuous" the belief that such miserable human materials could be transformed into acceptable citizens through the influence of American institutions and environment. Racial self-preservation clearly demanded restriction of immigration, and in the introduction to the fourth edition of his book in 1921 Grant observed with satisfaction that "one of the most far-reaching effects of the doctrines enunciated in this volume and in the discussions that followed its publication was the decision . . . to adopt discriminatory and restrictive measures against the immigration of undesirable races and peoples."

The racism preached by Grant and by popularizers like Lothrop Stoddard did play a decisive role in shaping the restrictive laws of the 1920s. Indeed, the principle of racial selectivity remained in force until the immigration law of 1965 abandoned the national-origins quota system. But as a scientific doctrine and a popular intellectual force, racism began to recede almost as soon as the national-origins system was enacted, and by the end of the decade the tide was clearly running against racism. Psychologists who had earlier interpreted the results of World War I army intelligence tests as confirming inborn racial differences shifted to an environmental explanation of the differences, and in anthropology the critique of racism mounted by Franz Boas and his students carried the day. Observation of the grotesque extremes of Nazi racism in the next decade and the revelation of its ghastly consequences during World War II utterly discredited racism as an idea and filled most Americans with repugnance for a theory so inhuman and opposed to democratic values.

Because of its identification with nativistic racialism, Anglo-Saxonism was also discredited. Although it had earlier been associated with liberal values, after 1930 Anglo-Saxonism seemed to intellectuals and social scientists the paradigm of narrow ethnocentrism. The term was not rehabilitated even by "consensus" writers of the 1950s who interpreted the American tradition more benignly than their "progressive" predecessors, and in the 1960s the acronymic WASP (white Anglo-Saxon Protestant) became the only ethnic slur permissible in enlightened circles. Like "melting pot" and "Americanization," the term "Anglo-Saxon" symbolized ideas and values that were contrasted unfavorably to "cultural pluralism."

Cultural Pluralism

The interpretation of ethnicity and American identity that came to be known as cultural pluralism was first presented in an article entitled "Democracy versus the Melting Pot: A Study of American Nationality," by Horace M. Kallen, which appeared in *The Nation* in February 1915. The article was reprinted in a collection of Kallen's essays (one of which was a passionate attack on the Americanization movement) called *Culture and Democracy in the United States* (1924), in which Kallen introduced the term cultural pluralism to designate his radically anti-assimilationist viewpoint. An early commentator, Isaac B. Berkson, writing before the term cultural pluralism was coined, in *Theories of Americanization* (1920) characterized Kallen as calling for a "federation of nationalities" in the United States, which is a fairly accurate expression of Kallen's position. He held that ethnic nationalities neither should nor could be transformed into any generic American nationality. Indeed, he affirmed that although there had been a unitary American nationality, it had been dissipated by the great waves of immigration, with the result that by 1915, America was not a nation with its own distinctive nationality but a political state within which dwelt a number of different nationalities. In these circumstances Kallen saw but two policy options: to work for unison or for harmony. He believed that the first option—the attempt to enforce conformity to a common pattern—would violate America's democratic ideals and the spirit of its institutions. Hence he recommended the goal of harmony, holding out the vision of "a possible great and truly democratic commonwealth."

> Its form would be that of the federal republic; its substance a democracy of nationalities, cooperating voluntarily and autonomously through common institutions in the enterprise of self-realization through the perfection of men according to their kind. The common language of the commonwealth, the language of its great tradition, would be English, but each nationality would have for its emotional and involuntary life its own peculiar dialect or speech, its own individual and inevitable esthetic and intellectual forms. The political and economic life of the commonwealth is a single unit and serves as the foundation and background for the realization of the distinctive individuality of each *natio* that composes it and of the pooling of these in a harmony above them all. Thus "American civilization" may come to mean the perfection of the cooperative harmonies of "European civilization"—the waste, the squalor and the distress of Europe being eliminated—a multiplicity in a unity, an orchestration of mankind.

This passage is the closest Kallen ever came to operationalizing the concept of cultural pluralism or to describing in practical terms the kind of situation its application would produce. Its extreme sketchiness and the obscurity of the language help explain why the idea is so hard to pin down and why the term was later used in so many different ways. It has always been more a vision than a rigorous theory.

Despite the vagueness and generality of Kallen's vision, several points are clear from the quoted passage and the discussion that preceded it. First, Kallen regarded his prescription as being more authentically American than the program of the Americanizers. Indeed, he saw cultural pluralism as the next logical stage of true Americanism, while forced-assimilation programs actually contravened American principles. According to Kallen, Americans were beginning to understand that "the political autonomy of the individual has presaged and is beginning to realize in these United States the spiritual autonomy of his group." But while there was growing appreciation of the fact that individual rights are fulfilled in group rights, this was by no means universally accepted by Americans. There was a real choice to be made between the two goals of unison or harmony. Kallen believed that unison could be achieved, but that to do so would require regimentation and controls that were incompatible with the basic law of the land and the traditional understanding of democratic procedures. The goal of harmony, on the contrary, was in line with realization that groups as well as individuals have rights and could usher in a "truly democratic" social order. While Kallen thus disagreed with the kind of program the 100-percent Americanizers espoused, he shared their convictions that the nation needed a positive policy in the area of ethnicity and national identity and that such a policy should be based upon the principles of the national ideology.

The second point to be underscored is that although Kallen envisioned a "democracy of nationalities" interacting within the same "federal republic," he was talking about cultural, not political, entities. Thus he spoke of the political autonomy of the individual giving rise to the spiritual (not political) autonomy of the group, and he portrayed the common political and economic system as furnishing the unitary foundation and background for the cultural realization of each distinctive *natio*. Kallen's pluralism was cultural because it dealt with such matters as the "emotional and involuntary life" of each group and the "peculiar dialect or speech . . . [the] individual and inevitable esthetic and intellectual forms" through which that life expressed itself. In 1924 Kallen dismissed critics who were disturbed about what he called "the irrelevant political suggestion of the word 'nationality.'"

But Kallen could not justly complain if people misinterpreted his position on the political status of "nationalities," because he left the entire political dimension woefully underdeveloped from the theoretical standpoint. He said nothing about why American principles did not demand the same respect for an ethnic nationality's political and economic autonomy as for its spiritual autonomy. He gave no hint as to how the legitimate cultural claims of a natio were to be distinguished from any inadmissible political claims, nor what political means a natio might employ in trying to obtain or protect its cultural rights. Kallen likewise failed to specify any concrete features of the political program that would be required to put his pluralistic vision on the road to realization, much less bring it to the multicultural perfection of an orchestration of mankind.

The failure to take up these obvious theoretical problems seems particularly puzzling in a man who was a professional philosopher and a disciple of the great pragmatist, William James. The best explanation for this curious deficiency is that Kallen was in this respect an optimistic idealist rather than a pragmatist. He simply assumed that these problems would take care of themselves if all efforts at cultural regimentation were abandoned by Americanizers and other melting-pot enthusiasts. Contemplating the world "with the benign gaze of a romantic," John Higham observes, "Kallen lifted his eyes above the strife that swirled around him to an ideal realm where diversity and harmony eternally coexist."

Besides being a romantic in the sense that he prized diversity and assumed that differences would automatically blend into cooperative harmonies, Kallen was also a romantic in his racialism. Because cultural pluralism came to be understood as liberal, anti-Anglo-Saxon, and antiracialist, it comes as a surprise to discover that Kallen shared the kind of romantic racialism represented by Anglo-Saxonism before it was absorbed into biological racism. Kallen's racialism was romantic in that he valued diversity as such and did not attempt to rank human groups as superior or inferior according to any absolute scale of racial merit. But he also resembled the romantics in attributing the distinctive characteristics of peoples to inborn racial qualities whose origin and nature were obscure. He did not discuss them in clear-cut biological or physical-anthropological terms, but "ancestry" played a crucial role, and even more central was a *Volksgeist*-like element of "inwardness."

In his 1915 essay Kallen spoke of respect for ancestors and pride of race as "primary and ultimate standards" and of a like-mindedness that was "inward, corporate and inevitable" because it sprang from "a homogeneity of heritage, mentality and interest." This like-mindedness, Kallen believed, was the necessary ground for the development of true freedom and equality, but it could not be generated by external conditions. Rather its "prepotent cause" was "a prevailing intrinsic similarity." Of the nationality of the immigrant Kallen wrote: "Behind him in time and tremendously in him in quality, are his ancestors; around him in space are his relatives and kin, carrying in common with him the inherited organic set from a remoter common ancestry. In all these he lives and moves and has his being. They constitute his, literally, *natio*, the inwardness of his nativity." Because the immigrant "cannot change his grandfather," his nationality could never change. Kallen concluded that "What is inalienable in the life of mankind is its intrinsic positive quality—its psycho-physical inheritance." This was a crucial point, for it was the inward and inevitable nature of immigrant nationalities that required their having full pluralistic scope for development.

Chided by Isaac Berkson for the emphasis on race in his 1915 article, Kallen was quite unrepentant in his 1924 book. He characterized his critics as laboring "to prove over again the well-known anthropological commonplace that race is a concept the underlying facts of which are contradictory," but at the same time he commended those who recognized the persistence and influence of heredity, and he insisted that "intermarriage or no intermarriage, racial quality persists, and is identifiable . . . to the end of generations." In

300 years intermarriage among white peoples in America had not produced a new race; rather the "older types" persisted, despite a superficial uniformity among all Americans accounted for by the school system, the mass media, and so on. Race, culture, family socialization, and nationality were all blurred together in Kallen's discussion. Concerning the "great tradition of Europe," he wrote: "Race, in its setting, is at best what individualizes the common [cultural] heritage, imparting to it presence, personality, and force." In some "vague . . . not well analyzed, and much misrepresented [way], race reacts selectively to culture"; hence, despite their other artistic accomplishments, the British were deficient in music, the Germans in architecture, the French in poetry. How were these temperamental differences between races perpetuated? Kallen seemed here to invoke a nonhereditary, family-socialization explanation. "Birth, which we do not choose," he wrote, "carries with it simultaneously certain cultural acquirements of a nature so basic, so primary, as to be indistinguishable from inheritance. The acquirements are, in fact, the infant's immediate social inheritance. They are the aboriginal impressions from the familial *milieu*." But Kallen did not systematically develop the distinction between biological and cultural inheritance, and his concluding statement brought physical inheritance again into prominence and linked race with nationality. All human associations, he stated, "have constituted communities tending to preserve and to sustain the continuity of the physical stock. Empirically, race is nothing more than this continuity confirmed and enchanneled in basic social inheritances. It is hardly distinguishable from nationality."

I have discussed at some length the racialist dimension of Kallen's original statement of cultural pluralism and his additional commentary in 1924 for several reasons. In the first place it is not widely known that racialism played any positive role in the tradition of cultural pluralism. Although Berkson drew critical attention to the racialist assumptions of Kallen's original formulation, cultural pluralism received very little attention of any kind for a number of years thereafter, and when it did begin to gain some currency in the late 1930s it was regarded simply as an attractively liberal and tolerant alternative to the melting pot or forced Americanization and was not associated in any way with racialism, which by that time had become much more disreputable.

Second, the racialist element was central to Kallen's argument that true democracy required cultural pluralism. Kallen believed that "the enterprise of self-realization," which it was the responsibility of democratic government to facilitate, could be successfully carried out only among groups whose members were inwardly like-minded, whose "inalienable selfhood" derived from common racial inheritance. From this it followed that democratic policy should "seek to provide conditions under which each [group] might attain the cultural perfection that is *proper to its kind.*"

Third, Kallen's racialism was also central to his conviction that ethnic nationalities would perpetuate themselves indefinitely. In this regard, he fully agreed with Anglo-Saxon nativists like Edward A. Ross, whose *The Old World in the New* (1914) apparently prompted Kallen's original article, and Henry Pratt Fairchild, who called the melting pot a "mistake" because "races" do not blend but go on being what they are despite the American environment. Kallen's conviction may also account for his failure to discuss the problem of *how* ethnic nationalities were to protect themselves from the inroads of assimilation, which had long been a danger to the integrity of ethnic cultures. This whole area is ambiguous, however, because although Kallen's language in the long passage quoted earlier indicates that he anticipated the indefinite perpetuation of ethnic phenomena, such as the mother tongue and societies, in another place he speaks of a group's undergoing changes but not losing its continuity, "even if it loses its memory." This seems to suggest that group identity would persist even after the loss of the cultural forms in which it expresses itself.

The fourth point to be emphasized is that Kallen's whole handling of race was extremely ambiguous. He was certainly not a strict biological racist like Madison Grant, but neither did he systematically distinguish between biological and cultural elements in the manner of Franz Boas. On the contrary, Kallen's discussion blurred the distinction Boas was trying to establish between a group's cultural heritage and its biological "continuity of physical stock." Moreover, Kallen talked about "nationalities" as embodying this undifferentiated inheritance in such a way as to make it virtually impossible to determine which elements of an ethnic group's identity were genetically determined and which were culturally transmitted.

Kallen never clarified these issues, and those who came after him in the pluralist tradition apparently failed to recognize them (except for Milton Gordon) and certainly failed to address them. Therefore the crucial role of Kallen's ambiguous racialist assumptions still constitutes a major theoretical problem in the cultural pluralist interpretation of ethnicity and American identity.

Kallen's assumption of automatic harmony among dozens of ethnic nationalities, each encouraged to develop its "spiritual autonomy" to the fullest, constitutes a second major theoretical ambiguity in cultural pluralism. Kallen himself simply postulated the elimination of the hatred and conflict that had historically marked the coexistence of different nationalities in Europe. He said nothing about how this happy circumstance was to be attained, and although later commentators denied that cultural pluralism would produce Balkanization and a clash of ethnic nationalities in the United States, none explained just what feature of the theory was to forestall such an eventuality.

Perhaps one reason these conceptual weaknesses have been so persistently overlooked is that Kallen's formulation did not attract wide attention for some time, and when the term cultural pluralism did gain currency, it was used very loosely and with small regard for what Kallen meant by it.

The most significant early notice came from Randolph Bourne, who acknowledged his debt to Kallen in a 1916 *Atlantic Monthly* article on "Trans-National America," and from Isaac Berkson and Julius Drachsler, who dealt more critically with Kallen's ideas in studies of assimilation published in 1920. These matters seemed less pressing, however, after the 1924 national-origins law virtually cut off the flow of European immigration. Thus, interest in assimilation and related issues began to wane almost precisely at the moment that Kallen introduced the term cultural pluralism. Those who did discuss cultural pluralism generally equated it with a liberal approach to Americanization—one that encouraged immigrants to retain their distinctive cultures during a period of initial adjustment, but anticipated eventual assimilation and the emergence of cultural unity.

By the late 1930s growing concern about prejudice and intergroup relations was reflected in Francis J. Brown and Joseph S. Roucek's compendious *Our Racial and National Minorities*, first published in 1937, reprinted in 1939, and revised in two later editions. Part IV was headed "The Trend toward Cultural Pluralism," but none of the authors in that section referred to Kallen, nor did his name appear in the 66-page bibliography. The section on cultural pluralism stressed the contributions made by Indians, Negroes, and immigrants to American culture, urged preservation of "the best that each group has brought," and noted the desirability of preserving "the fundamentals of [immigrant] heritages . . . for generations." Yet the writer who treated these matters most explicitly, E. George Payne, a prominent educational theorist at New York University, also denied that cultural pluralism meant "the ultimate preservation of different cultural streams in our civilization." Although he could see "no harm" in such a result, he regarded some degree of acculturation as inevitable and was confident that "a new and superior culture will emerge." Cultural pluralism, Payne concluded, "does not imply that the special cultures will continue unchanged in the general stream for all time.

The theory involves essentially a technique of social adjustment which will make possible the preservation of the best of all cultures . . ."

World War II added urgency to the task of improving intergroup relations. Cultural pluralism came into its own as a term designating both the actual existence of social diversity and the belief that such diversity was good, provided it was not accompanied by ethnocentrism, prejudice, or discrimination among the diverse groups. As it gained in popularity, however, cultural pluralism lost all semblance of conceptual rigor, becoming ever more vacuous and bland. Ostensibly it was an alternative to assimilation, but it implicitly assumed a degree of consensus sufficient to rule out serious tensions among groups. At the same time the growing tendency to employ the word pluralism (and derivatives such as pluralistic) without the modifier "cultural" made the concept all the more generalized and indeterminate.

Thus by the 1950s, cultural pluralism had become very popular and at the same time quite problematic as to content and meaning. I shall return to this matter in discussing the most recent period.

The most important point about the period 1860–1924 is that ethnicity assumed greater salience as an element in the national identity than it has had at any other time before or since. Especially during the first quarter of the 20th century, the ethnic factors of "race," nationality, language, and so on were the issues that sprang immediately to mind when Americans asked themselves, "What does it mean to be an American? What kind of Americanism do we want?" The four interpretations reviewed—the melting pot, Americanization, Anglo-Saxon racialism, and cultural pluralism—represent different ways of articulating the national self-understanding so as to answer those questions and at the same time indicate the general lines of policy that should be followed to realize the goals.

There were significant differences among the four perspectives, but they also overlapped with each other, which was inevitable in view of the elusive quality of matters relating to national identity. The four perspectives were subject to different interpretation because they had to be broad and multivalent in order to function as symbols for the processes and goals they represented. It should not be too surprising that the melting pot has been both equated with and contrasted to Americanization, or that some of the post-Kallen versions of cultural pluralism have been characterized as liberal Americanization and closely resemble a relaxed and tolerant version of the melting pot.

The four perspectives can be most usefully distinguished according to whether their inherent tendency is toward unity or multiplicity, whether they place greater stress on the *unum* or the *pluribus* in the national motto. The melting pot and cultural pluralism aspire to encompass both, but the former is assimilationist in tendency and assigns priority to unity, while the latter is antiassimilationist and, as originally articulated, looks to the preservation of a multiplicity of distinct ethnic nationalities. The melting pot envisions an overarching national culture and a distinctive American identity to which various ethnic cultures and identities would contribute, but into which they would be integrated as constituents, disappearing as separate cultural entities. *Pluribus* is thus taken into account, but is subordinated to and assimilated into *unum*. By contrast, Kallen's cultural pluralism leaves *unum* to take care of itself, so to speak, while making specific provision for *pluribus*, for the preservation of ethnic-cultural entities, not as contributors to a single distinctive national identity, but as equal partners in a pluralized, harmonious national identity.

Both Americanization and Anglo-Saxon racialism focused more exclusively on unity than did the melting pot. They had earlier been interpreted in a more liberal manner, but they came to mean that there was only one kind of acceptable American. Conformity to that version of cultural unity was required of all immigrants, who were not regarded as having anything valuable of their own to contribute to the national culture or identity. Americanization was more optimistic, because it assumed the immigrants could be systematically brought into conformity with the minimal requirements of Americanism; Anglo-Saxon racialism, however, finally denied that this was possible unless the immigrants were the right kind of racial material to start with. Americanization implied forced assimilation to one cultural pattern; racialism implied exclusion of all who did not already fit that pattern.

Just as these approaches may be ranged abstractly along a unity–multiplicity spectrum, their popularity or dominance can be aligned with the concern for unity at different times. Generally speaking, tolerant and inclusive versions of the melting pot, Americanization, and Anglo-Saxonism dominated during most of the 19th century, when national unity did not seem threatened by ethnic diversity. Uneasiness grew in the 1890s, however, as the flood of new immigration was coupled in the public mind with various forms of social, economic, and political unrest; during the crisis of World War I uneasiness became deep concern and was specifically linked with the dangers posed to national unity by the divided loyalties of "hyphenated Americans." In these circumstances faith in the automatic processes of the melting pot gave way, first to an active commitment to Americanization and then to a racialist-tinged despair over the nation's capacity to integrate the immigrants. Once restriction had been accomplished, Americans could afford to relax about national unity. They even became a little embarrassed about their former anxiety-induced narrowness and took a more benign view of cultural differences still existing. At this point, cultural pluralism began to gain general acceptance, but in a hazy form that differentiated it from assimilation much less sharply than when it was introduced by Horace Kallen.

Kallen's defense of multiplicity may also be understood as a response to the crisis of national unity in World War I. It seems clear that he was prompted to publish his pluralistic theory because of the extreme forms that the drive for unity was taking. At a time when members of ethnic minorities were being told, in effect, that they could not be good Americans if they continued to be who they were, it was fitting to articulate a philosophy of minority rights that justified their resistance to such campaigns and taught them that American principles could be marshaled in their defense. And perhaps cultural pluralism became less sharply differentiated from assimilation a generation later, not only because of *de facto* acculturation, but also because members of ethnic minorities were not subject to the same sort of insulting external pressures.

A final point about the salience of ethnicity as a dimension of American identity in this era concerns the central role played by Jewish immigration and Jewish intellectuals. The coming of about 2 million eastern European Jews between 1870 and 1914 made the Jews a numerically very significant element in the new immigration. Their visibility and impact was heightened by their concentration in New York City; in 1915 they numbered about 1.4 million and constituted 28 percent of the city's population. Antisemitism developed along with nativism and lent a special edge to the cultural pessimism of a patrician like Henry Adams or a racialist aristocrat like Madison Grant, both of whom despised Jews, while E.A. Ross lamented in *The Old World in the New* that Jews could not be made into good Boy Scouts! In the xenophobic 1920s, popular antisemitism was reflected in the Ku Klux Klan and fed by the calumnies circulated in Henry Ford's newspaper, the *Dearborn Independent*.

But far more important than the negative reaction against Jews was the positive role played by Jewish intellectuals who dealt with the question of ethnicity and American identity. Israel Zangwill and Horace Kallen were both Jews. Zangwill was English; Kallen, though German-born, had lived in the United States since early childhood. Both were highly self-conscious about their Jewishness: Kallen was a Zionist, and Zangwill, who was one of the founders of Zionism, broke with the majority in 1905 and founded the variant form known as "territorialism." Isaac Berkson and Julius Drachsler, early commentators on the melting pot and pluralism, were also Jewish and were specifically concerned with problems of Jewish survival and assimilation. Franz Boas, who did more than any other individual to refute racialism as a scientific doctrine, was also Jewish. And Randolph Bourne's adaptation of Kallen's ideas was an early milestone in the formation of the cosmopolitan, but heavily Jewish, New York intelligentsia.

In short, Jews played the same central role in the emergence of ethnicity as a salient element in the understanding of American identity that Catholics had earlier played in the emergence of religion as a prominent element. Blacks were to play a somewhat similar role in the next phase of the story.

Ethnicity Recessive and Resurgent (1924–1979)

Several of the terms and concepts reviewed in the previous section have continued in use to the present day, but their persistence is not the most notable feature of the era since the closing of massive overseas immigration. When considered as a unit, what is most striking about the past half-century is the ebbing and resurgence of ethnicity as a dimension of American identity. Two major themes interact; the first is the powerful reaffirmation of American ideology as the basis of national identity, which dominated the scene from World War II to the mid-1960s, and whose crests and troughs are inversely related to those of the ethnic impulse. The second is the issue of the status and condition of black Americans, which became increasingly central in the 1950s and 1960s, and whose evolution reveals most clearly the modulation from an ideological to an ethnic emphasis. Other features of the period that deserve attention are the explicit interest in the "American character" in the 1940s and early 1950s, and the growing involvement of social scientists (and to a lesser extent historians) in national-character studies and the resurgence of ethnicity, as well as in studies of blacks and the racial question.

Intense concern with ethnicity began to ebb in 1924. The national-origins law not only removed the issue from center stage politically, it also inaugurated an era in which the processes of assimilation gave the whole immigrant-derived population a more "Americanized" aspect. Ethnocultural passions played a prominent role in Al Smith's 1928 presidential campaign, but that contest proved to be a kind of epilogue to the period. The crash of 1929 and the Depression turned people's attention from cultural issues to elemental bread-and-butter concerns. National self-confidence rallied under Franklin D. Roosevelt, but neither New Dealers nor ordinary citizens gave much thought to ethnicity or national identity during the Depression decade.

The atmosphere of liberalism that prevailed under the New Deal did, however, encourage interest in intergroup relations in the later 1930s. The appearance of Brown and Roucek's 1937 book has already been noted; much other social science research was synthesized in William C. Smith's *Americans in the Making* (1939), significantly subtitled "The Natural History of the Assimilation of Immigrants." In history a cluster of outstanding works published between 1938 and 1941—Ray Allen Billington's *The Protestant Crusade*, Carl Wittke's *We Who Built America*, Marcus Hansen's *The Atlantic Migration* and *The Immigrant in American History*, and Oscar Handlin's *Boston's Immigrants*—marked a new level of visibility and sophistication for immigration historiography.

These historical works were sympathetic to the immigrant, but none of them claimed that ethnic groups had preserved their cultural identity in the pluralistic manner described by Kallen two decades earlier, nor did any of them imply that ethnic groups should do so. Insofar as they dealt with the matter at all, and allowing for differences of emphasis, these authors held to something like the classical version of the melting pot—that is, their accounts portrayed immigrant groups coming to the United States, meeting with various vicissitudes (including nativistic hostility), interacting with the host society, and eventually becoming part of that society, while at the same time contributing to it something distinctive from their own heritage. Like the subtitle of William Smith's book, the subtitle of another excellent historical work, Theodore Blegen's *Norwegian Immigration to America: The American Transition* (1940), epitomized the assumption of scholars of that era that they were describing a process of Americanization, the gradual blending of many diverse elements into one people.

All tendencies to underscore Americanism and national unity were massively reinforced by the entry of the United States into World War II. Indeed it would be difficult to exaggerate the importance of the war as the central event in shaping Americans' understanding of their national identity for the next generation.

On the level of practical social reality, the war was a great common experience, especially for the 12 million young men and women who served in the armed forces, but also for the whole population, which shared "for the duration" anxieties, privations, losses, hopes, and in the end, exhilaration. The feeling that "we're all in this together" was strong, inconceivably so to the Vietnam War generation. The typical war movie featured an Italian, a Jew, an Irishman, a Pole, and assorted "old American" types from the Far West, the hills of Tennessee, and so on, and this motif was not confined to Hollywood. The same image of military life as a kind of melting pot appeared in the winter 1942 issue of *Common Ground*, a journal put out by the Common Council for American Unity, which was dedicated to strengthening national cohesiveness by improving mutual understanding among the diverse groups in the population. Participation in the war effort gave even the newest immigrants a livelier sense of belonging to the national community. Howard Stein and Robert Hill in *The Ethnic Imperative* (1977), emphasize the significance of wartime experiences in broadening the horizons and hastening the assimilation of second- and third-generation immigrants in the Pittsburgh area.

Even more important was the accentuation of the ideological basis of American identity that accompanied the wartime crisis. This development was perfectly understandable in view of the challenge posed by the rise of totalitarianism and the frightening spectacle of Nazi arms sweeping across Europe. As Carl Becker acknowledged in vindicating "some generalities that still glitter" in 1940, it was Nazism that "brought into strong relief [democracy's] essential virtues," even for those, like Becker himself, who had previously found much to criticize in American democracy. In these circumstances, Americans were sensitized to ideology, as noted in 1943 by one of the keenest students of intergroup relations, Robert E. Park. They became highly self-conscious affirmers of their own system of values, having been galvanized to a fresh appreciation of freedom, equality, and the other principles of American democracy by the monstrous contrast of Nazism.

The implications of this ideological reawakening for ethnicity and its relation to national identity were brought out clearly in the statement of purposes on the inside cover of *Common Ground*, edited in its first year and a half by Louis Adamic. The Common Council for American Unity (known earlier as the Foreign Language Information Service) listed the first of its purposes as:

> To help create among the American people the unity and mutual understanding resulting from a common citizenship, a common belief in democracy and the ideals of liberty, the placing of the common good before the interests of any group, and the acceptance, in fact as well as in law, of all citizens, whatever their national or racial origins, as equal partners in American society.

The statement called for appreciation of the contributions of each group, for tolerance of diversity, for the creation of an

American culture "truly representative" of all the people, for an end to racial or ethnic prejudice, and for assistance to immigrants or their children who encountered difficulties in adjusting to American life.

Here ethnicity and pluralism of a sort were taken seriously into account. But although they were portrayed as important features, they were not the basic elements of the national identity. Rather it was identification with a set of universal ideas and values that made Americans what they were, despite differences of race, religion, or national background. Acceptance of all groups on an equal basis and tolerance of ethnic diversity derived as corollaries from "a common belief in democracy and the ideals of liberty." They were crucial corollaries, to be sure, but they were derivative from, not constitutive of, the essence of Americanism.

The need to emphasize both the ideological core and the ethnic-tolerance corollary was particularly pressing when *Common Ground* began publication in the fall of 1940. An "Editorial Aside" in the first issue explained the reasons: "We begin in difficult times. Never has it been more important that we become intelligently aware of the ground Americans of various strains have in common . . . that we reawaken the old American Dream, the dream which, in its powerful emphasis on the fundamental worth and dignity of every human being, can be a bond of unity no totalitarian attack can break." American entry into the war made unity all the more imperative, further heightening the stress on the commitment to freedom and democracy that bound all Americans together. And despite the prominence given to the "from-many-lands" motif, ethnicity was in fact compromised as a legitimate principle of group cohesiveness because of its kinship to the racialism and *völkisch* nationalism of the Nazis. The term ethnicity had not yet come into use as a designation for group belongingness or a "sense of peoplehood," but ethnocentrism was very widely used and its connotations were wholly negative; it meant the kind of group consciousness that expressed itself in feelings of superiority toward others and inspired prejudice and discrimination. The urgent wartime need was to eliminate this kind of ethnic consciousness on the basis of the democratic ideology.

The prefatory remarks to the second and third editions of Brown and Roucek's volume bear witness to the predominance of the ideological theme. Both of these editions, published in 1946 and 1952, respectively, carry the main title *One America* as a testimony to the authors' conviction that "in the crucible of war we are moving toward a cultural democracy. We have become and will remain One America." The substitution of the term "cultural democracy" for "cultural pluralism" made explicit the ideological basis of the appeal for unity and ethnic tolerance. In 1952 Brown and Roucek insisted that deeper understanding of the roots of America's heterogeneity was required if ethnocentrism was to be avoided and "if democracy is to be a living reality for each of the 150,000,000 people who make up our population." The third edition also showed that the cold war continued, indeed sharpened, the ideological accent. Because "the problems of America's minorities [were] problems of world minorities," the nation's performance took on new significance. "The degree to which we achieve equality of opportunity for each American is of international consequence for it is a basic propaganda weapon in the struggle between democracy and communism. Ideals, no matter how effectively portrayed, are counteracted even by isolated manifestations of prejudice and discrimination." Race relations was the crucial area in this respect.

The growth of interest in "the American character" in the 1940s and 1950s had two sources, both associated with World War II. Generically it was part of the intense curiosity about the United States and American culture that resulted from the nation's new role as one of two global superpowers and as the bastion of the values of Western civilization. In this sense, American character studies may be thought of as part of the broader American studies movement that grew up in the postwar years, not only in the United States but also in Europe and elsewhere.

More specifically, studies of the American character were inspired by, and represented one variety of, investigations of national character by social scientists working for the U.S. government during the war. Margaret Mead, author of one of the best-known examples of the genre, *And Keep Your Powder Dry* (1942), later explained that she and other anthropologists were called upon by defense agencies to apply their skills to such questions as how civilian morale might be maintained under various conditions, such as bombing attacks, how friction between the British people and American troops could be minimized, what policies were best calculated to persuade the German or Japanese people to accept surrender, and so on.

In dealing with inquiries like these, Mead and her colleagues attempted to apply "at a distance" (without direct observation of the peoples involved) the techniques worked out in the 1930s by the culture-and-personality school of anthropology. Mead was one of the leaders of this school, which combined psychoanalytic assumptions about the crucial importance of infantile and childhood experience with ethnographic studies of child rearing and socialization patterns to identify the "basic personality structure" produced by the social needs and cultural norms of particular groups. "By the end of the war," Mead wrote in 1961, "the term 'national character' was being applied to studies that used anthropological methods from the field of culture and personality, psychiatric models from psychoanalysis, statistical analysis of attitude tests, and experimental models of small-group process."

The development of national-character studies is relevant to our concern with American identity for several reasons. Most obviously, it stimulated interest in the subject and made that interest more explicit. Before 1940 most commentary on national character was a by-product of discussions on history, religion, literature, or some other subject, written, for the most part, by humanistically inclined writers. When social scientists took up the question of national character during the war, it became an object of "scientific" study, and its lingering disreputability because of the previous connection with racial theories was removed. Now the national character was associated with a method of investigation that was regarded as the best hope of solving the problems confronting society.

It is of particular interest that Erik Erikson was associated with the social scientists engaged in wartime national character studies. His book *Childhood and Society* (1950) appeared at the height of the enthusiasm for such studies, and a chapter entitled "Reflections on the American Identity" was perhaps the first example of the use of the term identity in such a context. In the same book Erikson explicitly connected ethnicity with identity in the passage quoted at the beginning of this essay.

Erikson was not alone in associating ethnicity and identity. The immigrant experience also figured prominently in Mead's *And Keep Your Powder Dry* and Geoffrey Gorer's *The American People* (1948). Both writers employed an assimilationist perspective in that they obviously assumed that in the lives of immigrants Americanization had been a much more significant reality than preservation of ancestral cultures. Indeed, both writers focused on assimilation as the paradigmatic dimension of immigrant experience for understanding the American character. For Gorer the immigrant's rejection of the European past was paradigmatic; for Mead it was the ambiguities of third-generation status.

Gorer's first chapter, "Europe and the Rejected Father," opened with the immigrants' being required to give up their past and transform themselves into Americans. Those who immigrated as adults were unable fully to do so and hence became objects of disdain to their American-born children, who rejected them as role models and authority figures. "It is this break of continuity between the immigrants of the first generation and their children of the second generation which is . . . of major importance in the development of the modern American character," according to Gorer, who generalized along Freudian lines to account for Americans' rejection of authority, the minimal familial role of fathers as compared to mothers, and so on.

Much of this had been anticipated by Mead, although she did not stress the Freudian implications so strongly. References to the immigrant experience recurred throughout her book, and its ruling interpretive metaphor was developed in a chapter entitled "We Are All Third Generation." Mead's point was not so much that many Americans actually were third-generation immigrants, but that "most of us—whatever our origins—[are] third-generation in character structure . . . [because] we have been reared in an atmosphere which is most like that which I have described for the third generation." Mead summed up the third-generation mentality as follows:

> Father is to be outdistanced and outmoded, but not because he is a strong representative of another culture, well entrenched, [and] not because he is a weak and ineffectual attempt to imitate a new culture; he did very well in his way, but he is out of date. He, like us, was moving forwards, moving away from something symbolized by his own ancestors, moving towards something symbolized by other people's ancestors . . . And to pass him it is only necessary to keep on going and to see that one buys a new model every year. Only if one slackens, loses one's interest in the race towards success, does one slip back. Otherwise, it is onward and upward, *towards* the world of Washington and Lincoln; a world in which we don't fully belong, but which we feel, if we work at it, we some time may achieve.

The ideological note, as in the reference to Washington and Lincoln, was strong, because Mead's aim was to marshal scientific self-understanding for the tasks of winning the war and building a better world. She was sensitive to the tensions between democracy and a social-engineering approach, but concluded that the two were compatible. "Those social behaviors which automatically preclude the building of a democratic world must go," she stated categorically; social science could contribute to this effort, it seemed, by showing how antidemocratic attitudes and institutions could be changed with the greatest possible tolerance and humanity.

The ideological dimension of the book is of considerable interest, especially because Mead recognized and dealt explicitly with the problem of the limits of tolerance. But the point that is most pertinent here is that for her, as for Gorer, the person of immigrant derivation was a prototypically American figure, not because of any distinctiveness of cultural heritage, but for exactly the opposite reason, because the ethnic exhibited in extreme degree the "character structure" produced by the American experience of change, mobility, and loss of contact with the past. This interpretation was consistent with the picture of the immigrant experience portrayed in Oscar Handlin's *The Uprooted* (1951), doubtless the most widely read and influential book on immigration history. Published at the height of interest in the American character, *The Uprooted* began with the author's assertion that "the immigrants *were* American history," and the central metaphor of uprootedness could be applied to Americans generally. Handlin made the point explicit in his last chapter: "The newcomers were on the way toward being Americans almost before they stepped off the boat, because their own experience of displacement had already introduced them to what was essential in the situation of Americans."

Although it ended on the positive note that migration meant liberation and that uprootedness had called forth new creative energies, Handlin's moving portrayal of the immigrant's alienation and his elegiac tone gave *The Uprooted* a place in the literature of existentialist and mass-culture criticism of American society. Existentialist criticism dwelt on the rootlessness and alienation of modern man, his irrational fears and anxieties. The mass-culture theme, which often overlapped the existentialist, focused on the shallowness and superficiality of an "other-directed" people who were unduly preoccupied with material success and status symbols, conformist in attitude and thought, and easily aroused to hysterical outbursts of nativism, anti-intellectualism, or anti-Communism. Both types of criticism flourished mightily at mid-century.

All these themes—the ideological revival, the belief that immigrants were the archetypical Americans, and the existential and mass-culture critiques—interacted in shaping the highly elusive and contradictory understanding of pluralism and diversity that obtained in the 1950s. That understanding seemed to be that although Americans were a pluralistic people, they did not have much real diversity; they therefore needed more, but this diversity must never be divisive.

The first two assumptions reflected the belief that although immigrants came from many lands, the later generations were not only Americans all but had Americanized so thoroughly that they were fast becoming an indistinguishable part of a bland, homogenized, and conformist society. The conviction that America needed more diversity followed from the cultural critique as a remedial prescription and also grew out of the democratic commitment to tolerance; if diversity disappeared, would that not imply that we had been untrue to the principle of tolerance? But the diversity so much desired could not be of the sort that divided Americans against each other in any serious way. In respect to ideology, the limits of permissible diversity were sharply demarcated. Un-Americanism in the 1940s and 1950s was ideological rather than religious or ethnic. But religion too was an area where diversity had limits: one of the standard arguments in the controversy over public aid to parochial schools was that such schools were "divisive." It was an argument that carried weight even with liberals who bemoaned the homogenization of American life and regarded the anti-Communist crusade as a betrayal of American principles.

It is within this context that we can best approach two significant books of the period, Horace Kallen's *Cultural Plural-*

ism and the American Idea (1956) and Will Herberg's *Protestant-Catholic-Jew* (1955).

Kallen's book, consisting of three lectures by the author, overwhelmingly favorable comments by nine other scholars, and a reprise by Kallen, was his first important statement on the subject since the 1920s. The volume, intended as the first in a series of studies in human relations to be published by the University of Pennsylvania, symbolized the degree to which cultural pluralism had become the conventional touchstone of enlightened wisdom. The fact that Kallen was invited to initiate the series also indicated that he had been rediscovered as the father of cultural pluralism. But Kallen's 1950s cultural pluralism was very different from what it had been 30 years before. All hint of racialism had disappeared, but so had the specifically ethnic quality of cultural pluralism, which now embraced the "diverse utterances of diversities—regional, local, religious, ethnic, esthetic, industrial, sporting and political . . ." And Americanization, which had been a movement to be resisted in the 1920s, had been replaced by an "Americanization, supporting, cultivating a cultural pluralism, grounded on and consummated in the American Idea."

Kallen's extremely diffuse notion of cultural pluralism implied a specific philosophical understanding of democracy, which he called "the American Idea." The longest essay in the collection was devoted to a Whitmanesque roll call of its prophets, symbols, doctrines, and the documents that constituted "the Bible of America." In replying to R.J. Henle, a Roman Catholic critic who challenged Kallen's tendency "to regard Americanism as an ultimate ideology, to make it a surrogate religion, and to identify it with cultural relativism," Kallen's language revealed how much his thinking had been affected by the ideological revival of World War II:

Of course, then, the [American] Idea isn't a "surrogate" to any religion. Nor is it a substitute for all. It is that apprehension of human nature and human relations, which every sort and condition of Protestant, Catholic, Judaist, Moslem, Buddhist, and every other communion must agree upon, be converted to and convinced of, if they mean to live freely and peacefully together as equals, none penalizing the other for his otherness and all insuring each the equal protection of the law. And this is how the American Idea is, literally, religion.

In the 1950s Kallen was as insistent as ever on pluralism, but it was pluralism bounded by a universally required commitment to Americanism, understood in quasi-religious terms.

Will Herberg, a "Judaist," approached the matter from a diametrically opposite position in his book. He meant to repudiate the tendency to erect "the American Idea" into what came to be called a civil religion in the 1960s. The situation needed unmasking, in Herberg's view, because traditional religionists had been misled by the contemporary revival of religion into thinking that their churches were gaining strength and influence, whereas they were in fact being reduced to the status of functionally useful supporters of "the American Way of Life,"—the *real* religion of Americans.

Herberg began with the paradox that America was simultaneously experiencing a great revival of religion and a continuing growth of secularism. To explain this, he turned to the social psychology of an immigrant-derived people, suggesting that the resurgence of the churches resulted from the desire of third-generation immigrants to reestablish contact with their ancestral heritage. This inclination had first been noted by Marcus L. Hansen, and Herberg gave the name "Hansen's Law" to the formulation, "What the son wishes to forget, the grandson wishes to remember." According to Herberg, the religious dimension of an ethnic heritage was best suited for third-generation remembering for several reasons. First, it had persisted more successfully than other dimensions of immigrant culture, such as language, which had been almost completely eroded by assimilation. Second, the religious traditions had been Americanized and now suited the mentality of the third generation. Third, religion provided an effective vehicle of social identity by providing an answer to the question, "Who am I?" Finally, religion, which was much prized in American society, offered an attractive linkage to the past, whereas foreign "nationality" was not only fading away but was also suspect as a form of ethnocentrism.

Herberg thus portrayed the religious revival as deriving largely from the fact that religion served as a kind of residuary legatee of ethnic feeling. But why did the view that religion was good enjoy such widespread support in American society? Why did leading public figures like President Eisenhower insist so strongly that religion was indispensable to national well-being? The reason, Herberg said, was that the American ideology itself was a spiritual construct embodying such values as freedom and individual dignity, as well as more mundane elements associated with material progress, and it had always been closely associated with religion. In the early days it had been intertwined with Protestantism, but with the coming of the immigrants and the adjustment of their religious traditions to the new environment, Catholicism and Judaism took their places beside Protestantism as "the three great faiths of democracy." Hence Protestantism, Catholicism, and Judaism were socially praiseworthy because they constituted three equally acceptable ways for the individual to manifest his commitment to the "spiritual values" underlying the American way of life. Herberg greatly admired the American ideology, but he steadfastly opposed the tendency to erect it into a civil religion. No traditionally believing Christian or Jew, he said, could acquiesce in the view that religion was a good thing primarily because it furnished the spiritual underpinnings for a secular ideology.

Herberg's critique is particularly interesting as a contrast to Kallen's elevation of the American idea to religious status. Even more pertinent here is that both writers placed ideological consensus at the center of American identity, even though Kallen was considered the prophet of cultural pluralism, and Herberg stressed an ethnic explanation for the religious revival and drew attention to the fact that American religion had actually been pluralized, or at least trinitized.

The ideological element was equally prominent with respect to race relations, and what has already been said about the influence of World War II applies in this area too. Systematic study of race relations was hardly a decade old when the Carnegie Corporation in 1937 commissioned a massive investigation of the situation and prospects of the American Negro and selected the Swedish social scientist, Gunnar Myrdal, to direct the project. The enormous collaborative effort was completed the year after Pearl Harbor and appeared in 1944 as *An American Dilemma*. The dilemma was that the treatment of blacks in the United States was in direct contradiction to what Myrdal called "the American Creed," to which he believed Americans were genuinely committed, despite their sorry record of racial prejudice and discrimination.

Myrdal's concluding chapter, "America Again at the Crossroads," drew together several strands of argument and analyzed with remarkable prescience the forces that were to revolutionize race relations in the next generation. After stating that the war was crucial for Negroes and was bound to bring about a redefinition of their status, Myrdal reviewed the social trends that had brought the racial situation to the point that the war would have that effect. The most important was the gradual destruction of the theoretical basis for race prejudice, which was now regarded as a mark of ignorance. This development robbed white people of confidence and troubled their conscience, but it heartened black Americans, who were becoming better educated, more self-conscious, and more assertive. Myrdal summed up the state of affairs on the eve of World War II as follows:

America can never more regard its Negroes as a patient, submissive minority. They will continually become less

well "accommodated." They will organize for defense
and offense. They will be more and more vocifer-
ous . . . They will have a powerful tool in the caste
struggle against white America: the glorious American
ideals of democracy, liberty, and equality to which
America is pledged not only by its political Constitution
but also by the sincere devotion of its citizens. The Negroes are a minority, and they are poor and suppressed,
but they have the advantage that they can fight whole-
heartedly. The whites have all the power, but they are
split in their moral personality. Their better selves are
with the insurgents. The Negroes do not need any other
allies.

This was the shape of things when World War II broke
out. Myrdal's assessment of its effect on the situation also
deserves quotation:

This War is an ideological war fought in defense of
democracy. The totalitarian dictatorships in the enemy
countries had even made the ideological issue much
sharper . . . than it was in the First World War. Moreover, in this War the principle of democracy had to be
applied more explicitly to race. Fascism and nazism are
based on a racial superiority dogma—not unlike the old
hackneyed American caste theory—and they came to
power by means of racial persecution and oppression.
In fighting fascism and nazism, America had to stand
before the whole world in favor of racial tolerance and
cooperation and of racial equality . . . It had to pro-
claim universal brotherhood and the inalienable human
freedoms.

The war thus accelerated "an ideological process which was
well under way," stimulated Negroes to exert greater pressure for change, and redoubled the discomfiture of white
Americans at their failure to abide by the principles of freedom and equality in the area of race.

In the midst of this "dramatic stage of the American caste
struggle," Myrdal unerringly identified "a strategic fact of

utmost importance . . . that the entire caste order is extra-legal if not actually illegal and unconstitutional." The Jim Crow laws of the South were only a partial exception, because "even they are written upon the fiction of equality" in the form of separate but equal treatment. The idea of legalizing a color-caste system on a national basis was never entertained, Myrdal declared, because that would be too radical a repudiation of the American creed.

Caste may exist, but it cannot be recognized. Instead, the stamp of public disapproval is set upon it, and this undermines still more the caste theory by which the whites have to try to explain and justify their behavior. And *the Negroes are awarded the law as a weapon in the caste struggle.* Here we see in high relief how the Negroes in their fight for equality have their allies in the white man's own conscience. The white man can humiliate the Negro; he can thwart his ambitions; he can starve him; he can press him down into vice and crime; he can occasionally beat him and even kill him; but he does not have the moral stamina to make the Negro's subjugation legal and approved by society. Against that stands not only the Constitution and the laws which could be changed, but also the American Creed which is firmly rooted in the Americans' hearts.

On the basis of this analysis of the situation, Myrdal urged Americans to seize the opportunity presented for reform, for the principal conclusion of his study was that *"not since Reconstruction has there been more reason to anticipate fundamental changes in American race relations, changes which will involve a development toward the American ideals."* Developments in race relations over the next generation testify to the astonishing acuity of Myrdal's insight in apprehending the imminence of change, in identifying the factors that would bear upon it, in singling out the resort to law as a key weapon in the struggle, and above all in insisting that the ideological issue was uppermost and that stressing it would win the conscience of white society as an ally in the cause. Without depreciating other factors or glossing over the ugly resistance engendered, it seems indisputably clear that growing consciousness of the flagrant discrepancy between American ideals and American racial practice was the crucial point of leverage in the civil rights phase of the black movement, from World War II through the mid-1960s. During these years the ending of separate-but-equal and the drive for desegregation of schools and public accommodations brought the democratic ideals of freedom and equality together with the goal of an integrated society in which black and white might intermingle freely on the basis of common citizenship and mutual adherence to the values of the American creed. There were great differences between the situation of blacks and that of "national" minorities, but blacks too were embraced within the vision of One America, a nation made up of diverse peoples who were tolerant of each other and united around a set of universalist values.

Because race was the most important issue in American domestic life in the early 1960s, any shift in the relative weight of ethnic, as distinguished from ideological, considerations in this area was bound to have a profoundly influential effect on national thinking. Such a shift occurred in the mid-1960s and presaged a much wider revival of ethnicity that was clearly noticeable by the end of the decade.

No specific dates can be confidently assigned to changes of this nature, but two events in 1965 and one in 1966 may be taken as symbolic indications of the reorientation that was under way. Two pieces of legislation passed in 1965—the civil rights act of that year and the immigration law that eliminated national origins as a principle of selectivity— stand as climactic achievements of the approach that had emphasized universalist principles to improve intergroup relations and create a better social order. By contrast Stokely Carmichael's dramatic introduction of the slogan "Black Power" in 1966 symbolized the emergence of a much greater emphasis on particularistic group consciousness, pride, cohesiveness, and assertiveness, which is associated with the enhanced salience of ethnicity in American public life both as an issue in debates about social policy and as a dimension of our national self-understanding.

Ethnicity had been a factor in these matters before 1966, and ideology continued to make itself felt after that date. What changed was the relative weight given to these two elements. From the mid-1960s there was not only a much greater positive stress on ethnicity, but also a passionate critique of the national ideology that discredited the older Americanist emphasis. Against the background of the Vietnam War and the racial crisis, Myrdal's language about the American creed or Kallen's about the American idea seemed inappropriate, to say the least. The revival of ethnicity thus was part of a deep crisis of confidence and self-respect among the American people. In reviewing this most recent phase of the interplay between ethnicity and American identity, we must therefore consider not only the growth of ethnic consciousness but also the weakening of the ideological element.

Social scientists were calling attention to the development of stronger ethnic feeling among blacks by the early 1960s. Reviewing race relations in the 20 years since the publication of *An American Dilemma,* Robin Williams reported in 1965 that "a stronger sense òf common fate, of shared values, beliefs and interests and of collectivity obligations" had undoubtedly emerged among blacks since 1944. Three years earlier another sociologist had described the process of "ethnogenesis" at work among blacks since emancipation, especially in the 20th century. As these studies were published, whites were being eliminated from leadership positions in the civil rights movement, and increasing black militance was fueled by the successes already won and by the solidarity engendered by the violent outbursts of urban rioting. After 1965 pride of race manifested itself not only in a new self-designation—"black" instead of "Negro"—but also in the purposeful promotion of black power, black pride, black history, black studies, and black consciousness, with black separatism and the paramilitary Black Panthers representing the extreme positions. The great mass of American blacks never supported the more extreme versions of militance, clinging instead to the ideals of equality and integration that had been emphasized in the earlier civil rights phase. However, they welcomed the new sense of group pride and dignity, for they had never regarded integration as a process that required them to deny their own identity.

The effects of this shift toward an "ethnic" emphasis by blacks were enormous. The first of three distinguishable effects was that it legitimated the reality of ethnocentrism, although it did not legitimate the term. "Ethnocentrism" had been used pejoratively for so long that it was irredeemable as a label, which may be why the new term "ethnicity" gained popularity so rapidly in the late 1960s and early 1970s. But the new attitude pioneered and legitimated by blacks was ethnocentric in the literal sense that it was strongly centered on group membership, group solidarity, and group interests, and in the further sense that it made these dimensions of group existence normative; a thing was judged to be good or bad according to whether it strengthened or weakened the group, furthered or hindered its interests. The claims of the group were equated with the requirements of abstract justice, and hostility to outsiders was justified on the grounds of this coincidence between group interests and universal justice.

American blacks could argue with a good deal of plausibility that justice sustained their group claims, but the legitimation of ethnocentric assertion of group claims could not be restricted to blacks. And because blacks seemed to be getting a great deal by the militant statement of such claims, backed up by group pressure and even by violence or the threat of violence, other groups naturally followed suit. This widespread imitation may be thought of as the second way in which the ethnic revival among blacks affected the general social scene. Chicanos and American Indians could also make strong claims on the national conscience, and they soon emulated the blacks with Brown Power and Red Power movements.

The "white ethnic" movement was conditioned by both of the factors already mentioned, but it also reflected a third effect of the black movement: it was systematically promoted as a way of defusing white backlash. The danger that white working-class resentment of black pressures would intensify racial strife had been recognized as early as 1964. But not until 1968, *after* the black legitimatization of ethnicity, was there the beginning of a movement to depolarize the situation by attending sympathetically to the complaints of the white working class and by encouraging their sense of ethnic identity and expression of ethnic aspirations. The connection was made quite explicit at a Consultation on Ethnic America held in New York in June 1968 and at a similar gathering two weeks later in Philadelphia. The American Jewish Committee was the principal organizer of these events and remained actively engaged in the white ethnic movement. In 1970 its ongoing National Project on Ethnic America was announced and designated a Depolarization Project. The same intention to persuade white ethnics that blacks were their allies was observable in the community-organization aspect of the white ethnic movement. The fact that it was promoted as an effort to reduce racial tensions helped to make foundation support available.

Although the influence of the black assertion of ethnicity was very great, it could not have had such an effect if there had not been a pool of latent ethnic consciousness among other groups. In other words, the revival of ethnicity represented a positive development by other segments of the population, as well as an imitation of, and reaction to, developments among American blacks. The positive quality of the ethnic affirmation was especially notable among Mexican Americans and other Hispanics because these groups are large, still strongly attached to their language and culture, and heavily reinforced by the continuing arrival of first-generation immigrants. But the work of historians and sociologists who dealt with older groups is also instructive because it reflected growing interest in the subject of ethnicity and showed that ethnicity was persisting much more tenaciously than earlier students had assumed it would.

The most important institutional center for immigration history in the 1950s was Harvard University, where Oscar Handlin guided a number of able scholars into the field. John Higham, who did his doctoral work at Wisconsin, published his rich study of American nativism in 1955, and in 1961 the Cornell-trained Lee Benson pioneered in "ethnocultural political analysis" in *The Concept of Jacksonian Democracy*, a critique based on close study of New York State. The ethnocultural approach in political history was carried further in the 1960s by scholars like Frederick Luebke, Richard Jensen, and Paul Kleppner, while Stephan Thernstrom, a Handlin student, introduced a new approach to the quantitative study of immigrant social mobility in *Poverty and Progress* (1964). In 1965 the first steps were taken toward organization of the Immigration History Society, and Timothy L. Smith set up an archive for materials relating to immigration at the University of Minnesota. At about the same time Rudolph J. Vecoli (who later became the director of the Minnesota Immigration History Research Center) published the first widely noted essay by a historian challenging the assumption that immigrants had been radically uprooted from their ancestral culture, suggesting by implication that they had preserved much more of their ethnic heritage than scholars had previously believed.

The same point had been made with greater impact in two books by social scientists: Nathan Glazer and Daniel Moynihan's *Beyond the Melting Pot* (1963) and Milton Gordon's *Assimilation in American Life* (1964). The former analyzed the persistence of group self-awareness and distinctive patterns of group culture among the Negroes, Puerto Ricans, Jews, Italians, and Irish of New York City and showed how this kind of ethnicity influenced upward social mobility and the political life of the city at large. Glazer and Moynihan's title and the statement that the melting pot "did not happen" implied that the authors denied the reality of assimilation, but their point was actually more subtle. Assimilation was real, and cultural pluralism in the federation-of-nationalities sense was "as unlikely as the hope of a 'melting pot.'" But "the assimilating power of American society and culture operated on immigrant groups in different ways, to make them . . . something they had not been, but still something distinct and identifiable." In their view, stated in italics, "*The ethnic group in American society became not a survival from the age of mass immigration but a new social form.*" Ethnicity, then, persisted, but it was transformed in the process.

Like Glazer and Moynihan's book, Gordon's study is too complex and nuanced to be adequately characterized in a few lines. From the viewpoint of later developments in the ethnic revival, however, two features stand out. First, Gordon's lengthy and knowledgeable review of earlier assimilation theories became the standard treatment of the subject. Second, he clarified and elaborated an important distinction between cultural pluralism and structural pluralism. Although he and other writers had outlined this distinction in the 1950s, *Assimilation in American Life* established its significance more fully. According to the distinction, cultural pluralism meant that an ethnic group maintained distinctive cultural features, such as language and customs, whereas structural pluralism meant merely that the members of the group interacted socially with each other more than they did with outsiders. Gordon believed structural pluralism was replacing cultural pluralism; although ethnic languages and customs were disappearing, the members of groups that had earlier been distinguished by these cultural markers still interacted with each other more frequently than they did with persons who did not belong to the group.

Gordon's work appeared too soon after Glazer and Moynihan's to permit him to comment on their assertion that ethnicity persisted but was transformed. His notion of structural pluralism was quite compatible with their argument, however; in fact, the two interpretations reinforced and illuminated each other. Both were also compatible with the influential suggestion by Fredrik Barth in 1969 that in studying ethnic groups the primary focus should be on "the ethnic *boundary* that defines the group, not the cultural stuff that it encloses." Thus by 1970, when the ethnic revival was getting under way, scholars had refined their earlier conceptions of assimilation and acculturation; they were coming around to the view that ethnicity was a more durable quality than they had previously supposed, and they were prepared to credit the possibility of its expression in novel or unexpected forms.

The themes of ethnic persistence *and* transformation are present in the work of the sociologist Andrew M. Greeley, a Roman Catholic priest and director of the Center for the Study of American Pluralism at the National Opinion Research Center, who has been prominently associated with the new ethnicity on the academic and scholarly front. The same is true of Michael Novak, a Roman Catholic layman of Slovak descent who approaches the subject of ethnicity in a more personal manner. Novak's *Rise of the Unmeltable Ethnics* (1972) remains the major manifesto of the movement.

These spokesmen sometimes stress that the new ethnicity really is *new* and not a carryover from immigrant nationalities of the past, but that is not the impression conveyed by the movement as a whole or by the rhetoric employed by its advocates. In fact, quite the opposite impression is conveyed by the constant reiteration that the melting pot never happened, that assimilation was a myth, that Americanization was a repugnant but futile effort to force everyone into the mold of "Anglo-conformity," that the nation was in the beginning, is now, and ever shall be "unmeltably" ethnic, and that those who called themselves the Americans were only another ethnic group—the WASPs—who lorded it over everyone else for far too long, but who have finally been unmasked.

This brings us to the other dimension of the ethnic revival, the fact that it is dialectically related to the weakening of the ideological element in American identity, which was so dominant in the epoch of World War II. There is a paradox here, for the advocates of the new ethnicity have not, of course, repudiated the principles of freedom, equality, and democracy. Indeed, they insist that their position conforms to the requirements of these principles more adequately than does the assimilationist mentality that they assail. Nonetheless, their approach implicitly denies that there can be a unitary *American* identity based upon common assent to universalist principles, an identity that makes Americans *one people* despite differences of ethnic derivation. And to treat terms like Americanization, assimilation, and melting pot as hateful labels for reprehensible policies—as the spokesmen for the new ethnicity consistently do—inevitably implies that the nation never represented values and ideals that immigrants could reasonably accept, identify with, and defend.

Although Americanization and the melting pot acquired unfavorable connotations around World War I, that is not the principal source for the intensely negative usage of these terms in the revival of ethnicity. As we have seen, even Horace Kallen spoke favorably of Americanization in the 1950s, and Will Herberg's popularization of the "triple melting pot" almost restored that much-maligned symbol to respectability. Rather, it was the events of the 1960s that discredited Americanism and made it possible, even fashionable, for ethnic spokesmen to treat these terms as wholly opprobrious.

The racial crisis and the Vietnam War, which had the opposite effect of World War II, were clearly the two most important forces that called American values and institutions into question. Closely related were revolutionary New Left radicalism and the counterculture that repudiated virtually all the values traditionally associated with American life. Radical feminism reinforced the tendency to reject traditional values. And in the Watergate scandal of the early 1970s, those who had cast themselves as true patriots and defenders of the old-fashioned virtues further weakened public confidence in American institutions and severely damaged national self-respect. No brief review could do justice to these tangled developments; it will be sufficient simply to highlight a fundamental shift of assumptions about America and to show how this shift is related to the subject of ethnicity and national identity.

The traditional position was that the American system was good and that Americans were committed to it, even though they did not fully live up to its ideals. Myrdal had elaborated the critique implied by this set of assumptions as it related to race relations, and the civil rights movement incorporated the same assumptions. For although they charged that the American people were hypocrites, the leaders of the civil rights movement acted on the premise that the nation really believed in equality and that its legal and political system offered the means that would, in the end, bring about racial justice. Outside the racial area, President Kennedy was able to appeal to patriotism without embarrassment and mobilized youthful idealism for service to the world through the Peace Corps.

A decade later the situation had changed drastically. The view that America was systemically oppressive and immoral was not the majority view, but it had been advanced so vehemently by numerous partisans and acquiesced in so tamely by authoritative figures that national confidence and self-respect were severely shaken. Both domestic and foreign policy were castigated, not merely as wrong, but as evil and obscene, not as the results of incompetence or human error, but as the inevitable products of a fundamentally vicious system. Although the critics differed over whether the root of the evil was racism, imperialism, militarism, fascism, or simply capitalism, they concurred in the view that "AmeriKKKa," as the most extreme radicals phrased it, was built upon oppression. The American creed, according to this interpretation, had never been anything but a sham; the American dream had always been a nightmare; democratic procedures were but a smokescreen, and the ideal of law and order merely a code term for the preservation of a system of exploitation manipulated by the establishment.

Although sketched here in fairly drastic form, a critique along these lines found wide acceptance among an intelligentsia that was particularly sensitive to the racial issue and historically susceptible to the appeal of romantic anticapitalism as proclaimed by the neo-Marxist New Left and by certain apolitical elements of the counterculture. Anti-Americanism of this intensity was always a minority position, but it represented in grotesque caricature the self-doubt and self-disgust Americans felt as they beheld the nation mired down in an ignoble foreign war and torn apart by racial violence, political assassinations, gunplay and riotous confrontation on college campuses, as well as scandal in the highest reaches of government. The decade 1965–1974 thus witnessed a severe weakening of confidence in the American system—in the principles on which it was based, in the integrity of those who espoused such principles, and in the efficacy of its institutions.

This crisis of confidence was more than just the background against which the revival of ethnicity took place. It was also an indispensable element in the revival, for ethnic identities would never have been so vigorously affirmed if the ideological version of American identity had not been so tarnished. In these circumstances, it was highly functional for people to remember that they were really ethnic, simultaneously dissociating themselves from responsibility for the defects of the American system and establishing a claim against those who were responsible—the WASP establishment. In many cases, the claim was basically for emotional restitution, but that was no small matter. And as national policy moved toward what Nathan Glazer has called "affirmative discrimination," ethnicity seemed on its way to becoming a criterion for the receipt of more tangible benefits. In the view of many observers, this development was well calculated to stimulate the ethnic revival even more by raising the stakes—that is, by rewarding those who successfully established a group claim for special treatment and punishing those who failed to establish such claims.

Like practically everything else associated with the new ethnicity, the point just mentioned is controversial, not merely in the sense that disagreements naturally arise over what ethnic groups, if any, are entitled to benefits, but also in that it implies what has been called an "optionalist" interpretation of ethnicity, which is at odds with the more traditional "primordialist" understanding. According to the latter view, ethnicity is a basic element in one's personal identity that is simply there as an inheritance from the past, one of the primordial qualities that enable an individual to situate himself in the world and that remain part of him no matter what. The contrasting optionalist view holds that ethnicity "may be shed, resurrected, or adopted as the situation warrants," because it is not some indelible stamp impressed on the psyche, but a dimension of individual and group existence that can be consciously emphasized or deemphasized as the situation dictates.

The conflict between these two interpretations goes to the heart of the relation between ethnicity and group identity, but I cannot attempt to evaluate it here, and I cannot pursue the development of the new ethnicity in greater detail. The revival of ethnicity is still too new, too much in process, to permit summary treatment, and any effort to provide an adequate description of the views of its advocates and critics would prolong the discussion unduly. Having reviewed the factors involved in the emergence of the new ethnicity and having shown how it contrasts with the ideological version of American identity, I will conclude with a few brief reflections on the evolution of American thinking about national identity.

Conclusion

Milton Gordon's definition of ethnicity as a sense of peoplehood is the simplest and most satisfactory yet proposed. It is
compatible with both of the interpretations of ethnicity
mentioned above, because a sense of peoplehood may be
conceived as either primordially given or optionally culti-
vated. But the way the term ethnicity is used has given rise
to a serious misunderstanding of the relationship between
ethnicity and American identity. The problem derives from
the fact that although Gordon's definition is theoretically generic (that is, it applies to any and all forms of the sense of
peoplehood), in practice the term is restricted to the sense of
peoplehood felt by subgroups within American society. Because ethnicity has become so closely associated with the
particularistic identities that differentiate the population in-
ternally, it has come to be regarded as qualitatively different
from American identity. This impression, which has established itself more or less inadvertently, is mistaken. If ethnicity is defined as sense of peoplehood, then the sense of
peoplehood shared by all Americans is *not* different in kind
from the sense of peoplehood shared by those Americans
who trace their ancestry to Italy, for example.

American identity and ethnic identity, then, are not two
different kinds of identity, although conventional usage implies that they are—and further implies that the latter is a
good deal more real and natural because it is a matter of
grandfathers and intimate personal associations. But while it
is generically the same, American identity differs from ethnic identity, as commonly understood, in two ways. First,
the sense of peoplehood that characterizes the national community is more inclusive than the peoplehood of ethnic
groups. Secondly, and precisely because it must be more inclusive, American identity has a more generalized formal
principle (namely, commitment to the universalist ideals of
Americanism) than those that form the bases of belongingness among ethnic groups. But the abstract quality of the

American ideology does not mean that American identity is without what might be called the grandfather effect. In the eight generations since independence, many series of grandfathers have revered the symbols of national loyalty, fought to uphold them, and thought of themselves as full-fledged Americans. Even for descendants of more recent immigrants, what Abraham Lincoln called the mystic chords of memory are intertwined with homes, and graveyards, in the new land, as well as with traditions from beyond the seas.

The generation of the founding fathers understood very well that building a new nation required the development of a national sense of peoplehood. They were quite self-consciously concerned over the establishment of what they called the national character. Because four out of five whites were of British derivation, because virtually all were Protestant, and because blacks and Indians were not considered part of the national community, Americans of that era may be considered highly homogeneous in culture. Dedication to freedom and self-government was an integral element in their British heritage and in their recent American experience, so there was naturally a close correspondence between the sense of peoplehood of the cultural majority (the founders, or core group, or WASPs) and the national sense of peoplehood they projected for the nascent republic. Yet American nationality was not simply "WASP ethnicity" writ large. On the contrary, it was regarded as something novel and distinctive; it was oriented toward the future rather than the past; and, most important, it rested on a commitment to universalist political and social principles rather than on particularist cultural features such as language, religion, or country of origin. Thus the ethnic consciousness-of-kind of the American core group was closely related to, but not identical with, the American nationality that was to be formed.

As the years went by, American nationality became more a reality and less a project for the future simply because of the accumulation of lived experience by people who thought of themselves as Americans. If the original mix in the population had continued without change, if there had not been massive immigration of culturally variant peoples, the original consciousness-of-kind of the core group would presumably have coalesced with American nationality in an unproblematic way—with the very large exception, of course, of the problem of where blacks and Indians fit in, which already existed at the founding and was not materially affected by immigration. But the coming of floods of immigrants who differed significantly from the cultural majority in language, religion, and country of origin raised intricate problems about the relation between American nationality and ethnicity. These problems were created, not just for the immigrating peoples, but also for the descendants of the founders, who had to articulate their tacit assumptions about the relation of American nationality to their own particularistic group sense.

This latter group—the WASPs in today's demeaning tag —could legitimately claim overwhelming credit for the establishment of the nation and the creation of its distinctive institutions, including its legal and political institutions. Not unnaturally, they had a proprietary sense about the nation and regarded themselves as the appropriate arbiters of what it meant to be an American. Yet spokesmen for the immigrating peoples could just as legitimately point out that becoming an American did not require one to become an Anglo-Saxon or even to be like an Anglo-Saxon, except in adhering to the principles of freedom, equality, and republican government and in repudiating all former political allegiance, accepting the Constitution, and obeying the laws.

In establishing American nationality on the basis of abstract social and political ideas, Protestant Americans of British background had in fact committed the nation to a principle that made it inconsistent to erect particularist ethnic criteria into tests of true Americanism, but they did not fully realize this at the outset. The growth of a large and culturally divergent immigrant population brought out into the open the tension between the universalist criteria of Americanism and the core group's natural desire to perpetuate the cultural hegemony of its own way of life. Hence the coming of the immigrants made the nature of American nationality problematic and required a rethinking of what it meant to be an American. Periods of intense concern over these issues, which generally took the form of nativism, may be understood as crises of nationality. This essay has shown that a difference in religion became the central issue in the first of these crises, while the crisis of the late 19th and early 20th centuries focused on so-called racial qualities. The drastic reduction of mass immigration in the 1920s ended that crisis, and the emphasis on democratic tolerance during World War II made nativism seem un-American, thus helping to pave the way for the positive valuation of ethnicity that emerged in the late 1960s.

It would overstate the case to call the contemporary revival of ethnicity a crisis of American nationality, yet it has made the question of what it means to be an American more prominent than it has been since the 1920s. Moreover, in the tradition of national debate on these matters, this is the first time that the affirmers of ethnicity have taken the offensive. The traditional Americanist position has not only been placed on the defensive, it has been left virtually undefended. However, it is by no means indefensible, and without depreciating the real gains in national self-understanding that we owe to the new ethnicity, that position is presently in greater need of a critique than is the traditional Americanist position. Such a critique might include two or three important points.

The first is simply that an American nationality does in fact exist. That it seems necessary to make such a statement indicates the degree to which the rhetorical imbalance of the recent discussion of ethnicity has created a situation in which very basic matters related to American identity appear questionable. For that reason it may not be redundant to add that American nationality is not Anglo-Saxonism or WASP ethnicity, nor is it a Kallenesque collocation of subgroup ethnicities taken together. Rather it is a distinctive sense of peoplehood, not different in essence from the peoplehood-sense of ethnic groups, which furnishes what Justice Felix Frankfurter once called "the binding tie of cohesive sentiment" underlying the "continuity of treasured common life" of the national community.

To affirm the existence of American nationality does not mean that all Americans are exactly alike or must become uniform in order to be real Americans. It simply means that a genuine national community does exist and that it has its own distinctive principle of unity, its own history, and its own appropriate sense of belongingness by virtue of which individuals identify with the symbols that represent and embody that community's evolving consciousness of itself. American nationality, so understood, does not preclude the existence of ethnicity in the subgroup peoplehood-sense, but neither does the existence of the latter preclude the former; nor should subgroup ethnicities be regarded as more privileged, as having some sort of existential priority over American nationality.

In the past, many ethnic nationalists explicitly denied that there was any such thing as American nationality, and Horace Kallen's original version of cultural pluralism rested on the assumption that, although at one time a distinctive American nationality did exist, it had been dissipated by the great waves of immigration. At present, however, the existence of an American nationality has been made questionable, not by flat denials of its existence, but more indirectly, as the result of rhetoric employed by spokesmen for the new ethnicity. One feature is the claim that the American people are simply a collection of ethnic groups, one of which—the WASPs—have oppressively dominated all the others and tried to impose Anglo-conformity. Harold Cruse, for example, has stated: "America is a nation that lies to itself about who and what it is. It is a nation of minorities ruled by a minority of one—it thinks and acts as if it were a nation of white Anglo-Saxon Protestants." And Michael Novak reported that Americanization "was really WASPification." Similarly, the repeated insistence that the melting pot "never happened" and that assimilation is a myth implies the nonexistence of American nationality, because that was what the melting pot was expected to produce and what immigrants were supposed to be assimilated to.

The standard rhetoric of the ethnic revival has also contributed to the erosion of confidence in the ideological principles upon which that nationality is based. That is not the intention of the ethnic spokesmen, to be sure, but respect for American principles cannot help but be weakened when the very words Americanism and Americanization are treated as terms of abuse and when earlier efforts to articulate the nation's values and to give them symbolic expression are dismissed as hypocrisy or worse. Polemical excesses were committed in the past by crusaders for 100-percent Americanism, but some contemporary champions of the new ethnicity are guilty of equal but opposite excesses. These excesses are potentially more destructive, however, because by undercutting respect for American values and institutions, immoderate criticism simultaneously erodes the ideological basis for the critics' claim for a fuller measure of justice. Claims for tolerance, equality, and justice must be based on the democratic principles of the national ideology, not on ethnicity as such. Spokesmen for the new ethnicity seem somehow to have forgotten that the particularistic sense of membership in a specific race, religion, or ethnic nationality in itself creates no claim on others for tolerance, respect, equality, or anything else.

To judge from current usage, one might infer that cultural pluralism meets all the points of the critique so far advanced. As customarily invoked, it seems to be regarded as a democratic principle of nationality that supplies a warrant in justice for all particularistic ethnic demands and guarantees that these multitudinous claims will not conflict with each other, but will automatically promote the common good and produce a harmonious and richer culture. Perhaps a theory of pluralism will eventually be worked out that will do all this—or that will at least provide an analytical perspective and conceptual tools to identify and deal with the real problems involved in maintaining unity and diversity, in reconciling the conflicting claims of the one and the many. Unfortunately, cultural pluralism today is not such a theory. It was filled with theoretical ambiguities when introduced by Kallen in the 1920s; as popularized in the 1940s and 1950s, it meant something quite different (even in Kallen's usage), and the ambiguities were multiplied. Against the background, the vicissitudes of the past 15 years or so have emptied cultural pluralism of theoretical coherence. Today it is not so much a theory as an incantatory expression that enables people to avoid confronting the need for a theory.

But the very popularity of the term, as well as the vigorous assertion of ethnic claims, bespeaks a real change in the Americans' sense of who they are and who they want to be. We need a better theory to deal with this than is presently available. What the new ethnicity and all the talk of pluralism signify is that the perennially problematic issue of American nationality is taking on a new configuration. It is a continuing task to make a reality out of the ideal proposed in the national motto—*E Pluribus Unum*. We cannot hope to settle the issue definitively, to finish the task once and for all. But we cannot even begin to do justice to the problem as it is posed in our own time unless we grant the same kind of recognition to the imperative of unity that we give to the reality of diversity.

BIBLIOGRAPHY

1. Concepts of Ethnicity

Early American theories of ethnicity include Robert E. Park, *Race and Culture* (Glencoe, Ill., 1950); Louis Wirth, "The Problem of Minority Groups," in Ralph Linton, ed., *The Science of Man in the World Crisis* (New York, 1945); and William Graham Sumner, *Folkways* (1906; reprint, New York, 1940). Gunnar Myrdal, *An American Dilemma* (1944; reprint, New York, 1975), a massive two-volume composite of interwar beliefs about Negroes, applied the assimilation doctrine to that minority. The analysis of assimilation was raised to a higher level of sophistication in Milton Gordon, *Assimilation in American Life* (New York, 1964).

Among the specifically historical works, those by Marcus Lee Hansen are especially valuable—*The Problem of the Third Generation Immigrant* (Rock Island, Ill., 1938; reprinted in *Commentary*, November 1952); *The Immigrant in American History* (1948; reprint, New York, 1964), a series of stimulating essays; and *The Atlantic Migration, 1607–1860* (Cambridge, Mass., 1951), the first of a projected three-volume series, never completed because of his premature death. Among other excellent works are Oscar Handlin, *Boston's Immigrants*, rev. ed. (New York, 1972); John Higham, *Strangers in the Land* (New York, 1963); Melville J. Herskovits, *The Myth of the Negro Past* (Boston, 1958).

Among the rather few works commenting on the formal counts by ethnicity, see two papers by William Petersen: "Religious Statistics in the United States," *Journal for the Scientific Study of Religion* 1 (1962): 165–178; and "The Classification of Subnations in Hawaii: An Essay in the Sociology of Knowledge," *American Sociological Review* 34 (December 1969): 863–877. A fascinating paper on a similar topic is Fulmer Mood, "The Origin, Evolution, and

Application of the Sectional Concept, 1750–1900," in *Regionalism in America*, 2nd ed., Merrill Jensen, ed. (Madison, Wis., 1965). The case for deleting "race" from the language is argued at length in Ashley Montagu, *Man's Most Dangerous Myth: The Fallacy of Race* (New York, 1964).

Of the recent flood of works on ethnicity, the following are recommended, partly for their excellence and partly because each represents a special emphasis lacking in blander texts: Brewton Berry, *Almost White* (New York, 1963); Nathan Glazer and Daniel P. Moynihan, *Beyond the Melting Pot: The Negroes, Puerto Ricans, Jews, Italians, and Irish of New York City*, 2nd ed. (Cambridge, Mass., 1970); Andrew M. Greeley, *Ethnicity in the United States: A Preliminary Reconnaissance* (New York, 1974); Einar Haugen, *Language Conflict and Language Planning: The Case of Modern Norwegian* (Cambridge, Mass., 1966); Harold R. Isaacs, *Idols of the Tribe: Group Identity and Political Change* (New York, 1975); Charles J. Levy, *Voluntary Servitude: Whites in the Negro Movement* (New York, 1968); and William Petersen, *Japanese Americans: Oppression and Success* (New York, 1971).

3. American Identity and Americanization

The brief section headed "Ethnicity and Identity" in *Ethnic Identity in Society*, Arnold Dashefsky, ed. (Chicago, 1976), provides a few hints toward a much-needed history of the term "identity." Of Erik Erikson's writings on identity, the most relevant to this subject are: "Reflections on the American Identity," in *Childhood and Society* (New York, 1950); "Identity and Uprootedness in Our Time," in *Insight and Responsibility* (New York, 1964); "Autobiographic Notes on the Identity Crisis," *Daedalus* (Fall 1970); and *Dimensions of a New Identity* (New York, 1974). Michael McGiffert, ed., *The Character of Americans*, rev. ed. (Homewood, Ill., 1970), is a collection of readings on the closely related concept of American character, and Thomas L. Hartshorne, *The Distorted Image* (Cleveland, 1968), traces the historical evolution of the concept of American character from the 1880s through the 1950s.

Hans Kohn, *American Nationalism* (New York, 1957), is basic for the ideological origins of American identity. Also very useful are: Paul Nagel, *This Sacred Trust* (New York, 1971); Michael Kammen, *A Season of Youth* (New York, 1978); Benjamin T. Spencer, *The*

Quest for Nationality (Syracuse, N.Y., 1957); and Merle Curti, *The Roots of American Loyalty* (New York, 1946). Robert A. Shalhope, "Toward a Republican Synthesis: The Emergence of an Understanding of Republicanism in American Historiography," *William and Mary Quarterly* (January 1972) is an excellent introduction to the recent scholarship on republicanism, and Lance Banning, *The Jeffersonian Persuasion* (Ithaca, N.Y., 1978), shows how republicanism influenced the political and ideological struggles of the early national period. For "civil millennialism," see Nathan O. Hatch, *The Sacred Cause of Liberty* (New Haven, Conn., 1977).

Thomas T. McAvoy, *A History of the Catholic Church in the United States* (Notre Dame, Ind., 1969), provides a general account of Catholic developments, 1815–1865; Jay P. Dolan, *The Immigrant Church: New York's Irish and German Catholics, 1815–1865* (Baltimore, Md., 1975), is a valuable social history. Ray Allen Billington, *The Protestant Crusade 1800–1860* (New York, 1938), the standard account of ante-bellum nativism, is nicely supplemented by Robert F. Hueston, *The Catholic Press and Nativism 1840–1860* (New York, 1976), which concentrates on the Catholic reaction. Oscar Handlin's landmark study, *Boston's Immigrants*, rev. ed. (Cambridge, Mass., 1959), illuminates the special quality of Catholic-Protestant tensions in Boston. On the school issue, see Vincent P. Lannie, *Public Money and Parochial Education: Bishop Hughes, Governor Seward, and the New York School Controversy* (Cleveland, 1968), and Timothy L. Smith, "Protestant Schooling and American Nationality, 1800–1850," *Journal of American History* (March 1967). Philip Gleason, "Coming to Terms with American Catholic History," *Societas* (Autumn 1973), is a more wide-ranging review of Americanism and Americanization as issues in Catholic history.

John Higham's classic *Strangers in the Land* (New Brunswick, N.J., 1955) is indispensable for understanding the melting pot, Americanization, and Anglo-Saxon racialism; his *Send These to Me* (New York, 1975), chaps. 10 and 11, are crucial for cultural pluralism. Milton M. Gordon, *Assimilation in American Life* (New York, 1964) is also enlightening on these matters. Philip Gleason, "The Melting Pot: Symbol of Fusion or Confusion?" *American Quarterly* (Spring 1964), and "Confusion Compounded: The Melting Pot in the 1960s and 1970s," *Ethnicity* (March 1979), deal primarily with semantic issues. Maurice Wohlgelernter, *Israel Zangwill* (New

York, 1964), places *The Melting Pot* in the context of Zangwill's other writings.

On Americanization, see Edward G. Hartmann, *The Movement to Americanize the Immigrant* (New York, 1948); Daniel Weinberg, "The Ethnic Technician and the Foreign-born: Another Look at Americanization Ideology and Goals," *Societas* (Summer 1977); and John F. McClymer, "The Federal Government and the Americanization Movement, 1915–24," *Prologue* (Spring 1978). Lawrence A. Cremin, *The Transformation of the School* (New York, 1961), chap. 3, sets Americanization against the background of progressivism in education. For the involvement of employers, see Gerd Korman, *Industrialization, Immigrants and Americanization* (Madison, Wis., 1967).

Higham, *Strangers,* chap. 6, is the best short discussion of racism, but Reginald Horsman, "Origins of Racial Anglo-Saxonism in Great Britain before 1850," *Journal of the History of Ideas* (July/September 1976), is also extremely valuable, not only for its substantive content, but for its comprehensive citation of primary and secondary literature. Barbara M. Solomon, *Ancestors and Immigrants* (Cambridge, Mass., 1956), traces the rise of Anglo-Saxon racialism and nativism in New England. Thomas F. Gossett, *Race: The History of an Idea in America* (Dallas, Tex., 1963), is a useful general account. For eugenics and race, see Mark H. Haller, *Eugenics* (New Brunswick, N.J., 1963); for the critical work of Franz Boas, see George W. Stocking, Jr., *Race, Culture, and Evolution* (New York, 1968).

Critical commentaries on Kallen are few; the best are: Higham, *Send These to Me,* chap. 10; Gordon, *Assimilation in American Life,* chap. 6; and James H. Powell, "The Concept of Cultural Pluralism in American Social Thought, 1915–1965," Ph.D. dissertation, University of Notre Dame, 1971 (University Microfilms, Ann Arbor, Mich.). Moses Rischin, *The Promised City: New York's Jews 1870–1914* (Cambridge, Mass., 1962), is excellent for the social and cultural background of Jewish thinking on ethnicity and identity.

American thinking on ethnicity and identity in the period 1924–1979 has been little studied as a distinct subject. A number of works that constitute primary evidence of shifting views in this area are mentioned in the text and will not be listed here. Fred H. Matthews, *Quest for an American Sociology* (Montreal, 1977), makes a valuable contribution by focusing on the pioneering work of Robert E. Park and the "Chicago School." Park, *Race and Culture* (Glencoe, Ill., 1950), is a collection of his essays on these themes. Peter I. Rose, *The Subject Is Race* (New York, 1968), is helpful, as is Everett C. Hughes and Helen M. Hughes, *Where Peoples Meet* (Glencoe, Ill., 1952). Stanford M. Lyman, *The Black American in Sociological Thought* (New York, 1972), is also relevant here, especially for its chapter on Gunnar Myrdal and *The American Dilemma*.

Although Howard F. Stein and Robert F. Hill, *The Ethnic Imperative* (University Park, Pa., 1977), is primarily a critique of the new ethnicity, it also contains valuable evidence on the impact of World War II. For the war-related boom in studies of the national character, see the relevant chapters of Hartshorne, *Distorted Image*, and Margaret Mead's contributions to Daniel Lerner and Harold D. Lasswell, eds., *The Policy Sciences* (Stanford, Cal., 1951), and to Seymour M. Lipset and Leo Lowenthal, eds., *Culture and Social Character* (New York, 1961). Daniel Bell, "Modernity and Mass Society: On the Varieties of Cultural Experience," in *Paths of American Thought*, Arthur M. Schlesinger, Jr., and Morton White, eds. (Boston, 1963), offers a convenient entry to the cultural critique of the 1950s.

For perceptions by social scientists of changes among American blacks in the early 1960s, see L. Singer, "Ethnogenesis and Negro-Americans Today," *Social Research* (Winter 1962); and Robin M. Williams, Jr., "Social Change and Social Conflict: Race Relations in the United States, 1944–1964," *Sociological Inquiry* (Winter 1965). Rudolph J. Vecoli, "European Americans: From Immigrants to Ethnics," in *The Reinterpretation of American History and Culture*, William H. Cartwright and Richard L. Watson, Jr., eds. (Washington, D.C., 1973), is a comprehensive review of shifting emphases in historical scholarship on ethnicity. See also Richard L. McCormick, "Ethno-Cultural Interpretations of Nineteenth-Century American Voting Behavior," *Political Science Quarterly* (June 1974). Perry L. Weed, *The White Ethnic Movement and Ethnic Politics* (New York, 1973), is informative on the organizational development of the new ethnicity; Maxine Seller, *To Seek America; A History of Ethnic Life in the United States* (Englewood, N.J., 1977), chap. 13, offers a brief interpretive overview; and *America and the New Ethnicity*, David R. Colburn and George E. Pozzetta, eds. (Port Washington, N.Y., 1979), is a useful collection of readings.

For more theoretical discussions, see William L. Yancey, Eugene Ericksen, and Richard N. Juliani, "Emergent Ethnicity: A Review and Reformulation," *American Sociological Review* (June 1976), and Peter K. Eisinger, "Ethnicity as a Strategic Option: An Emerging View," *Public Administration Review* (January/February 1978), which discusses several recent works and suggests the distinction between the primordialist and optionalist views of ethnicity.